Chemistry Matters!

METALS AND METALLOIDS

Volume 6

Krista West

GROLIER

an imprint of

 SCHOLASTIC

www.scholastic.com/librarypublishing

About this set

Chemistry Matters! provides an intelligent and stimulating introduction to all areas of modern chemistry as reflected in current middle school and high school curricula. This highly visual set clearly explains principles and applications using dramatic photography and annotated artwork. Carefully chosen examples make the topic fun and relevant to everyday life. Panels detail key terms, people, events, discoveries, and technologies, and include "Try This" features, in which readers are encouraged to discover principles for themselves in safe step-by-step experiments at home or school. "Chemistry in Action" boxes give everyday examples of chemical applications.

First published in 2007 by Grolier, an imprint of Scholastic Library Publishing
Old Sherman Turnpike
Danbury, Connecticut 06816

© 2007 The Brown Reference Group plc

Volume ISBN 0-7172-6200-6; 978-0-7172-6200-7
Set ISBN 0-7172-6194-8; 978-0-7172-6194-9

Library of Congress Cataloging-in-Publication Data
Chemistry matters!
    v. cm.
  Includes bibliographical references and index.
  Contents: v.1. Atoms and molecules—v.2. States of matter—v.3. Chemical reactions—v.4. Energy and reactions—v.5. The periodic table—v.6. Metals and metalloids—v.7. Nonmetals—v.8. Organic chemistry—v.9. Biochemistry—v.10. Chemistry in action.
  ISBN 0-7172-6194-8 (set : alk. paper)—ISBN 0-7172-6195-6 (v.1 : alk. paper)—ISBN 0-7172-6196-4 (v.2 : alk. paper)—ISBN 0-7172-6197-2 (v.3 : alk. paper)—ISBN 0-7172-6198-0 (v.4 : alk. paper)—ISBN 0-7172-6199-9 (v.5 : alk. paper)—ISBN 0-7172-6200-6 (v.6 : alk. paper)—ISBN 0-7172-6201-4 (v.7 : alk. paper)—ISBN 0-7172-6202-2 (v.8 : alk. paper)—ISBN 0-7172-6203-0 (v.9 : alk. paper)—ISBN 0-7172-6204-9 (v.10 : alk. paper)
  1. Chemistry—Encyclopedias.
  QD4.C485 2007
  540—dc22
                    2006026209

For The Brown Reference Group plc
Project Editor: Wendy Horobin
Editors: Tom Jackson, Paul Thompson,
              Susan Watt, Tim Harris
Designer: Graham Curd
Picture Researchers: Laila Torsun, Helen Simm
Illustrators: Darren Awuah, Mark Walker
Indexer: Ann Barrett
Design Manager: Sarah Williams
Managing Editor: Bridget Giles
Production Director: Alastair Gourlay
Editorial Director: Lindsey Lowe
Children's Publisher: Anne O'Daly

Academic Consultants:
Dr. Donald Franceschetti, Dept. of Physics,
  University of Memphis
Dr. Richard Petersen, Dept. of Chemistry,
  University of Memphis

Printed and bound in Singapore.

Contents

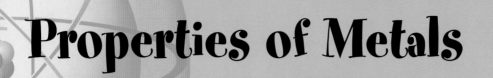

Properties of Metals

Most elements are metals, and we see them all around us, from a paperclip to the wings of a jet aircraft. Metals also form many important compounds. These substances are used to make dyes and soaps, and even occur in our bodies.

Nearly three-quarters of all the elements on Earth are metals. Many of the most common elements are metals, and they have been used by humans for thousands of years. Today modern technology uses metals to make everything from skyscrapers and spacecraft to medicines and paints.

People first began using metals to make tools about 5,000 years ago. Historians call that time the Bronze Age, because most metal objects were made of bronze. Bronze is a mixture of two metals: copper and tin. Bronze objects are not very strong but they still allowed people to create a wide range of tools to help them survive.

Metal cans are prepared to be filled with food. Metals are very useful substances and found in all areas of everyday life.

From about 1900 B.C.E., people began using a harder metal called iron. The Iron Age had begun. Iron tools and weapons were harder and more useful than bronze ones. Civilizations that could use iron were more successful than those still using bronze. People armed with iron weapons were able to defeat fighters equipped with bronze weapons.

During the Iron Age there were many migrations (movements of people) across Asia and Europe. As people learned to use iron, their civilizations became more powerful. As a result they began to take over new areas of land—all thanks to a metal. Iron is still the most-used metal today. Ninety-five percent of all metal objects are made from iron.

MEET THE METALS

There is no strict definition of a metal, but metals tend to have many similar properties: Metals are solid in normal conditions, and most only melt and boil at high temperatures. They are also shiny, flexible, and ductile—they can be stretched into thin wires. Metals are also good conductors. That is, they let electricity and heat pass through them quickly.

Of the 90 elements found naturally on Earth, 65 are metals. Iron (Fe) and nickel (Ni) are the most common metals on the planet.

Chemistry in Action

Colorful character

Some uses of metals are obvious, like electric wires and the bolts holding cars together. Others are not so clear, like the metals contained in colored items, such as lipsticks, dyes, and paints. Many of these get their color from metals. Some metals produce many different pigments (colored substances). For example, chromium produces yellow, red, and green pigments.

▼ *The colors of many paints are produced by substances that contain metal atoms.*

Seven of the elements are considered metalloids. These are substances with properties of both metals and nonmetals. They are sometimes termed semimetals. Silicon (Si) is the most common metalloid. One thing that makes metalloids different is that many are semiconductors. A semiconductor only conducts electricity in certain conditions. At other times they are insulators—they block the flow of heat and energy (*see* p. 60).

ORGANIZING THE METALS

Because there are so many different types of metals on Earth, chemists organize them in groups according to their atomic structure and properties. This helps chemists predict how different metals will behave when they encounter other elements.

The easiest way to learn the different groups of metals is with a periodic table, an organized array of the elements (*see* p. 45). The periodic table provides information about individual elements and groups of elements. Metals are found on the left-hand side of the table, and

Earth's super-hot core is thought to be made of these metals. In the rocks of Earth's crust, aluminum (Al) is the most common, followed by iron, sodium (Na), potassium (K), and magnesium (Mg). Like most other metals, these elements occur as ores. An ore is a natural compound, or mineral, that contains large amounts of a metal. (A compound is a substance that is formed when the atoms of two or more elements join during a chemical reaction.) A few metals, such as gold and silver, are found pure instead of as ores.

The other metals must be refined from ore. A refined metal has been purified to get rid of other unwanted elements. Once pure, most metals are then used in alloys. An alloy is a metallic substance that is made up of two or more metals mixed together. For example, brass is an alloy of copper and zinc.

▲ *A statue made from bronze, a mixture, or alloy, of two metals— copper and tin. Bronze objects have been made for 5,000 years, and the alloy is still a useful material today.*

Key Terms

- **Alloy:** A metallic substance that contains two or more metals.
- **Metal:** An element that is generally solid, shiny, moldable, ductile, and conductive.
- **Metalloid:** A substance with properties of both a metal and a nonmetal.
- **Refine:** To purify a metal by getting rid of other unwanted elements.
- **Ore:** A mineral that contains valuable amounts of a metal.

Chemistry in Action

Stardust

Scientists think that just three elements —hydrogen, helium, and lithium—were created 14 billion years ago in the first moments of the Big Bang. Hydrogen and helium gases were most abundant, but there were also tiny amounts of the metal lithium. Lithium is the lightest of all metals, and also has the smallest atom. It floats in water and oil.

▶ Lithium is the simplest metal. It is found in the huge clouds of gas and dust that form into stars.

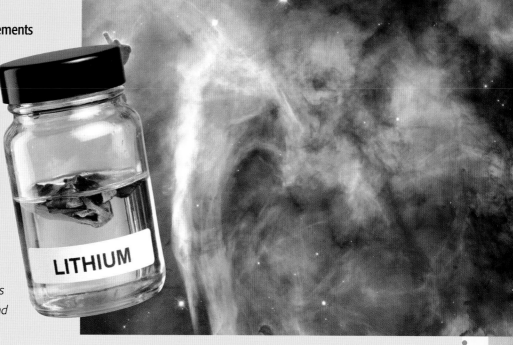

nonmetals on the right. Most elements are considered metals, so they spread more than halfway across the table.

The periodic table is used to show chemists trends among the elements. The most metallic elements are located in the bottom-left corner. The most nonmetallic ones are positioned in the upper-right corner. The boundary between metals and nonmetals is a diagonal line running through the left side of the table, from aluminum (Al) to polonium (Po).

In the periodic table elements are formed into columns. A column of elements is called a group. Each group has a number that shows where the column sits in the table.

The atoms of the members of a group have a similar structure. It is this structure that determines how an element will react and form bonds. This book examines five types of metals.

INSIDE METALS

All elements, including the metals, are made of atoms. Atoms are the smallest pieces of an element that can retain the properties of that element. The structure of the atom is important because it determines how that element bonds with other elements. How an element forms bonds determines many of the properties of that substance. Let us back up a little and review the inside of the atom.

▼ *Pure silicon looks a little like metal. However, this element is a metalloid and it has some of the properties of both metals and nonmetals.*

At the center of the atom is the nucleus, a dense ball of positively charged particles called protons and neutral particles called neutrons.

The protons give the nucleus a positive charge. Opposite charges attract each other, while the same charges repel (push away). As a result the nucleus attracts negatively charged particles called electrons. These move around the nucleus. It is an atom's electrons that are involved in reactions.

GIVING AND TAKING

The electrons move in layers called shells that surround the nucleus. Larger atoms have more electrons than smaller ones. Their electrons are arranged in larger shells. Electrons fill the shells outward from the nucleus. The smallest shell is closest to the nucleus. The next shell

▼ *All metal atoms have only a few electrons in their outer electron shells. The atoms of a few metals have three or four outer electrons, but nearly all metal atoms have just one or two electrons. The low number of outer electrons makes metals behave and react in similar ways.*

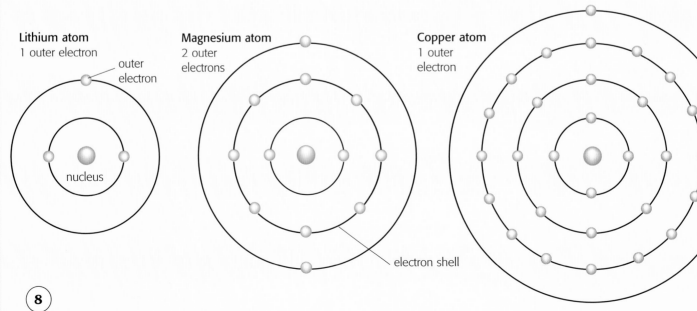

Lithium atom
1 outer electron

outer electron

nucleus

Magnesium atom
2 outer electrons

electron shell

Copper atom
1 outer electron

Key Terms

- **Atom:** The smallest unit of an element.
- **Bond:** An attraction between atoms.
- **Electron shell:** A layer of electrons that surrounds the nucleus of an atom.
- **Element:** The simplest type of substance made up of just one type of atom.
- **Nucleus:** The central core of an atom containing protons and neutrons.
- **Valence electrons:** The outermost electrons of an atom; they are involved in chemical reactions.

is larger and contains more electrons; each new shell is farther from the nucleus and larger.

The electrons that reside in the outermost shell—the valence electrons —are the ones involved in chemical reactions. The number of an atom's valence electrons determines how that atom forms bonds with other atoms.

When an atom forms a bond, it gives, takes, or shares electrons in an effort to become stable. A stable atom is one where the outer shell is either full of electrons or empty. An atom with a nearly full outer shell will not give away its electrons easily. Instead it will gain electrons from other atoms to become stable. An atom with only a few outer electrons will give them away easily. That makes its outer shell empty and the atom stable.

Nearly all metals have atoms with just one or two valence electrons. (A handful of metals have three or four.) So metallic elements generally give away electrons to form bonds. This behavior is what makes metals all so similar.

History

Gold and greed

The Inca people lived in the Andes Mountains of Peru from 1438 to 1533. They constructed great cities of stone buildings in the mountains. Inca buildings are all the more amazing because they were built without metal tools. Incas could not purify copper or iron. Instead they used hard stones to make hammers, axes, and other equipment. However, Inca civilization used large amounts of another metal–gold. Inca people dug up pure gold, which they called the "sweat of the Sun." They used it to make cups, jewelry, and statues, but gold is too soft to make other tools. Gold was so common that it was not very valuable to the Incas. However, the first Europeans to come to Peru had different values.

Spanish explorers were the first to visit the Incas in 1532. The Incas presented their vistors with fine cloth, but the Spanish leader, Francisco Pizarro (circa 1475–1541), was more interested in their gold. After beating him in battle, Pizarro held Atahualpa, the Inca king, a prisoner until his people paid a huge ransom. The Incas filled one room with gold and two more with silver items, but Pizarro did not keep his side of the bargain and executed Atahualpa anyway.

▲ *An engraving from 1596 shows Inca people collecting gold to pay a ransom for their king, who had been captured by Spanish explorers.*

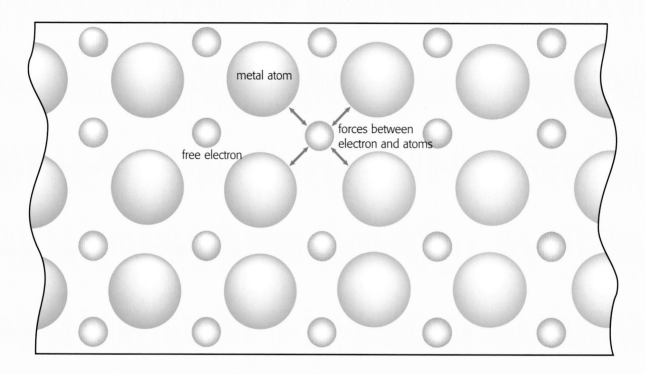

METALLIC BONDS

Metals are held together by metallic bonds. These bonds form when metal atoms share their outer electrons with each other. The outer electrons break off from the atoms and form a pool, or "sea," of electrons. The sea of electrons surrounds the metal atoms. Each free electron is attracted to the several nuclei around it. Because the particles are being pulled in all directions at once, the sea of electrons forms a "glue" that holds the metal atoms together.

The sea of electrons can flow through the metal. This ability gives metals many of their physical properties.

PROPERTIES OF METALS

As we have seen, metallic elements share similar atomic structures and they bond to each other in a certain way. As a result metals share many properties:

▲ Free electrons surround metal atoms. The electrons hold the atoms together in what is known as metallic bonding.

▼ Metals share many properties but there are also many differences between them. Mercury (1) is perhaps the most unusual metal because it is a liquid in normal conditions. Copper (2) has a red-brown color, while most metals are silver colored like magnesium (3).

- **Solid and shiny:** Tightly packed metal atoms form a solid and are able to reflect light well, making the metal appear shiny.

- **Flexible:** The sea of electrons that binds metal atoms can flow around. The atoms are not held firmly in one place, so metals can be bent or hammered into a new shape without breaking.

- **Ductile:** As a metal is stretched into a wire, the sea of electrons continues to flow around the atoms. As a result the metallic bonds can hold even thin wires together.

- **Conductive:** The sea of electrons is constantly moving. If the electrons are made to flow in one direction, they form an electric current.

- **High boiling and melting points:** Metallic bonds are strong bonds, so solid metals are generally tough solids. Strong bonds also require a lot of heat energy to break them so the solid can melt into a liquid and even more to boil a liquid metal into a gas.

REACTIONS OF METALS

Metals are reactive elements because they readily give or share their valence (outer) electrons. Two common chemical reactions involving metals are combination and displacement reactions.

▶ *The Statue of Liberty in New York Harbor is made of copper. It was built in 1886, and over the years the copper has reacted with chemicals in the air to make a blue-green compound called verdigris.*

During these reactions metals become ions. An ion is an atom that has lost or gained one or more electrons. Metal atoms lose their outer electrons and form positively charged ions. Atoms that gain electrons from metals during a reaction become negatively charged ions.

Ions with opposite charges are attracted to each other. This attraction creates a bond between the ions and forms an ionic compound.

Most ionic compounds form when a metal gives electrons to a nonmetal. A common example of an ionic compound is potassium chloride (KCl). It is created when potassium (K) bonds with chlorine (Cl). With one valance electron to give away, potassium reacts easily. Chlorine is a nonmetal gas. Its atoms need one electron to become stable. Put potassium and chlorine together, and potassium atoms will lose their outer electrons and give them to the chlorine:

$$2K + Cl_2 \rightarrow 2KCl$$

REACTIVITY

Some metals are more reactive than others. A reactive metal loses its outer electron or electrons more easily than a less reactive one. As a result metal atoms are often involved in displacement reactions. These occur when a reactive element replaces a less active element in a compound. For example, potassium is more reactive than calcium (Ca). So pure potassium will react with calcium chloride ($CaCl_2$) to produce pure calcium and potassium chloride. However, pure calcium is not reactive enough to displace potassium from its compounds.

▲ *A train wheel being made from hot steel. When hot, the metal is soft enough to bend and mold into shape. When it cools down, the wheel will be hard and very tough.*

Key Terms

- **Compound:** A substance formed when atoms of two or more different elements bond together.
- **Conductive:** Describes a substance that carries electricity and heat well.
- **Ductile:** Describes a solid that can be drawn into long wires without breaking.
- **Malleable:** Describes a material that can be pounded into a flat sheet.

Chemistry in Action

Reactivity series

Metals can be organized into a reactivity series—a list with the most reactive metals at the top and least reactive at the bottom. The reactivity of metals is determined by how easily their atoms lose their outer electron or electrons. The list below shows the reactivity of some familiar metals.

Potassium	K	
Sodium	Na	React with water
Calcium	Ca	
Magnesium	Mg	
Aluminum	Al	
Zinc	Zn	
Iron	Fe	React with acid
Tin	Sn	
Copper	Cu	
Mercury	Hg	
Silver	Ag	
Gold	Au	Unreactive
Platinum	Pt	

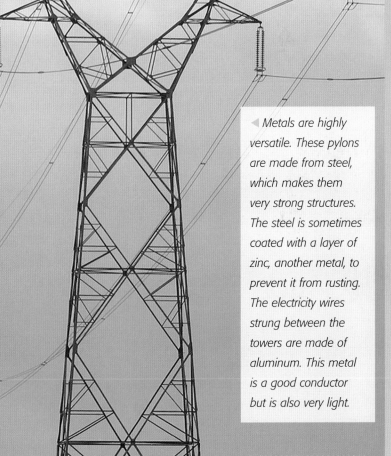

◄ Metals are highly versatile. These pylons are made from steel, which makes them very strong structures. The steel is sometimes coated with a layer of zinc, another metal, to prevent it from rusting. The electricity wires strung between the towers are made of aluminum. This metal is a good conductor but is also very light.

See Also ...
● Looking at Atoms, Vol. 1: pp. 24–35.
● The Metals, Vol. 5: pp. 34–43.

The Alkali Metals

Alkali metals are the most reactive group of metals. The most common alkali metals are sodium and potassium. These metals are included in many useful compounds, such as table salt, baking powder, and gunpowder.

The elements in Group 1, the first column on the left of the periodic table, are known as the alkali metals. The group includes six metals—lithium (Li), sodium (Na), potassium (K), rubidium (Rb), cesium (Cs), and francium (Fr). The first five of these metals were discovered in the 19th century when scientists figured out how to purify them from compounds found in nature. English chemist Humphry Davy (1778–1829) discovered potassium and sodium in 1807. Lithium was discovered by Swede Johann Arfvedson (1792–1841) in 1817. German Robert Bunsen (1811–1899) discovered cesium and rubidium in 1861. Francium was discovered in 1939, but it is the rarest element on Earth and very little is known about it.

Soap compounds contain the alkali metals sodium and potassium. The compounds form bubbles when mixed with water.

Chemistry in Action

Alkali-metal compounds

Compound	Formula	Common name	Use
Sodium chloride	(NaCl)	Table salt	Used to flavor food
Sodium bicarbonate	($NaHCO_3$)	Baking powder	Helps baked foods rise
Sodium hydroxide	(NaOH)	Lye	Used to make soap
Potassium carbonate	(K_2CO_3)	Potash	Used to make glass, enamel, and soap
Potassium chloride	(KCl)	–	Used as a plant fertilizer
Potassium nitrate	(KNO_3)	An ingredient of saltpeter	Used to make gunpowder and glass and to cure meat

▲ *A crop-dusting airplane sprays fertilizer on crops. Many plant fertilizers contain alkali-metal compounds.*

Though each chemist used a different method to discover the elements, they realized the new metals had a similar atomic structure and shared many chemical and physical properties. For example, the alkali metals, known as such because many of their compounds are alkalis (*see* p. 16), are much softer than most other metals.

ATOMIC STRUCTURE

The alkali metals have only one valence electron in the outermost shell (*see* p. 8). As a result they readily give away this electron to become more stable. Hydrogen also has one electron to give away and is sometimes included in Group 1. However, hydrogen is a gas in normal conditions and is not considered to be a metal.

It is their single outer electron that makes the alkali metals very reactive. A reactive element forms bonds with other atoms easily during chemical reactions.

ALKALIS AND ACIDS

Alkali metals are so called because they form compounds that are alkali. Alkalis are also referred to as bases. They are ionic compounds—made up of ions with opposite charges that are attracted to each other (*see* p. 19). Alkalis contain high numbers of negative hydroxide ions (OH^-). An alkali's positive ion is generally a metal. For example, sodium hydroxide (NaOH) is made of a sodium ion (Na^+) bonded to a hydroxide ion.

▶ *Pure sodium is soft enough to be sliced with a steel knife.*

▼ *Chemists test the pH of a substance using indicator paper. This paper changes color with pH. Alkalis make the indicator paper turn purple. Acids make the paper red. Neutral compounds make the paper green.*

| pH1 | pH2 | pH3 | pH4 | pH5 | ph6 | ph7 | pH8 | ph9 | ph10 | ph11 |

An acid is the opposite of an alkali. It has a high number of hydrogen ions (H^+). When an alkali reacts with an acid, the hydroxide and hydrogen ions combine to produce water (H_2O). The other elements in the acid and alkali compounds also form a product, which chemists call a salt. For example, sodium hydroxide and hydrochloric acid (HCl) react to form water and sodium chloride (NaCl). Sodium chloride is table salt, which is used to flavor food. This reaction is written like this:

$$NaOH + HCl \rightarrow NaCl + H_2O$$

Chemists measure the number of ions in acids and alkalis using the pH scale. A pH lower than 7 is considered acidic, and a pH higher than 7 is considered alkaline. Water has a pH of 7 so is neutral—neither acid nor base.

PROPERTIES

Because all of the alkali metals have a similar atomic structure, they also look alike and behave in the same way. Alkali metals have the following physical and chemical properties:

• **Soft:** All the alkali metals are soft enough to be cut with a steel knife. As the size and mass of an alkali-metal atom goes up, the metal gets softer. So the farther down the column on the periodic table, the softer the metal. For example, cesium is almost liquid at room temperature. The softness is due to weak metallic bonds (*see* p. 10). Alkali-metal atoms have just one electron each to form the sea of electrons, and the

A Closer LOOK

Purifying alkali metals

The alkali metals are very reactive. Although many of them are common in nature, they always occur combined with other elements to make compounds, such as table salt.

Chemists cannot extract alkali metals using chemical reactions and have to use electricity instead. An electric current separates the elements in certain compounds through a process called electrolysis (*see* vol. 3: p. 50). Even the most reactive elements, including alkali metals, can be separated in this way. However, more reactive elements require larger electric currents.

During electrolysis, positively and negatively charged rods are immersed in a liquid containing the compound to be split apart. Each rod attracts particles with an opposite charge, breaking the compound's bonds and separating the different ingredients.

This was the technique used by Humphry Davy in 1807 to purify first potassium and then sodium. That was the first time anyone had purified alkali metals. Davy used a simple battery called a pile to produce an electric current. Davy's assistant was Michael Faraday (1791–1867), who continued the study of electricity and later invented the electric motor.

▲ *A working model of the electrolysis equipment used by Humphry Davy to extract pure potassium from potash (potassium carbonate).*

electrons are spread thinly among the metal atoms. As a result the bonds that hold the atoms together are not strong.

Alkali metals with large atoms are more reactive than those with smaller atoms. In a smaller atom such as lithium, the outer electron is nearer to the nucleus. As a result the electron is held in place more strongly and is less likely to be involved in a chemical reaction. In a larger atom, such as one of potassium, the outer electron is held in place weakly and is more easily lost during a reaction.

• **Shiny and silvery:** All the alkali metals are shiny. Most are silvery gray, although cesium has a golden tinge.

• **Good conductors:** All the alkali metals conduct heat and electricity well.

• **Distinctive colors:** When the alkali metals are burned, they produce flames with characteristic colors. Lithium burns dark red, sodium is yellow, potassium is lilac, rubidium is also red, and cesium produces a blue flame.

• **Highly reactive:** The alkali metals are stored in oil so they do not react with oxygen in the air. Some reactions are so fast and intense that they create an explosion of heat and gas. Alkali metals

with large atoms are more reactive than the metals with small and light ones—large atoms lose their single outer electrons more easily during reactions.

BOND FORMATION
The single outer electron of the alkali metals is the key to how their atoms behave with other elements. To become

REACTIVITY →

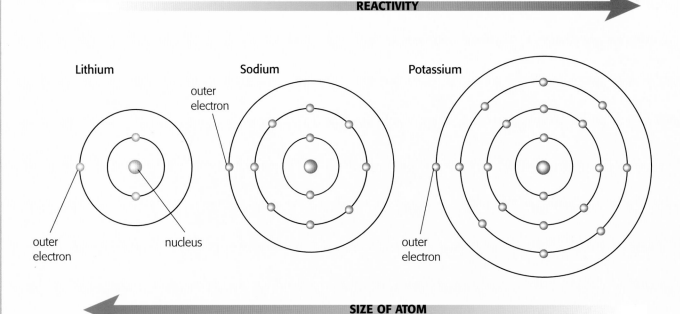

Lithium

Sodium

Potassium

outer electron

outer electron

nucleus

outer electron

← SIZE OF ATOM

stable, an alkali-metal atom must lose its single outer electron to empty its outer shell. It does this by forming an ionic compound.

An ionic compound is produced when a metal atom gives an electron to a nonmetal atom. The atom that gives away an electron loses a negative charge and becomes a positive ion. Chemists call positively charged ions cations. The atom that takes an electron receives an extra negative charge and becomes a negatively charged ion. Chemists call that an anion. The opposite charges of the cation and anion attract each other, which results in an ionic bond forming between them, creating a compound.

Sodium chloride is created in this way from sodium (Na) and chlorine (Cl). Sodium is a typical alkali metal. It has one electron to give away before becoming stable. Chlorine is a nonmetal gas in need of one electron to fill its outer shell and become stable.

Put sodium and chlorine in a container together, and sodium will lose its electron (becoming the cation Na^+) while chlorine takes the same electron (becoming the anion Cl^-). The Na^+ cation bonds with the Cl^- to form the compound NaCl, the chemical formula for table salt. The reaction is written as:

$$2Na + Cl_2 \rightarrow 2NaCl$$

FORMING ALKALIS

One of the most important reactions of alkali metals is with water. This is the reaction that produces the main alkali compounds for which the metals are named. In most cases the reaction is

violent, with the metal bursting into flames. Cesium reacts so explosively that it will shatter even a thick glass container.

As the least reactive alkali metal, lithium reacts with water more slowly. When you add lithium (Li) to water (H_2O), the metal atom combines with an oxygen and hydrogen atom from the water. Together they become a lithium cation (Li^+) and a

▲ *Potassium reacts with oxygen in the air and burns with a bright lilac flame. Only potassium produces flames of this color.*

hydroxide anion (OH⁻). These ions bond forming the alkali lithium hydroxide (LiOH). The hydrogen atoms left over from the water form into pairs (H_2). These hydrogen molecules are released as gas. The equation for this reaction is:

$$2Li + 2H_2O \rightarrow 2LiOH + H_2$$

SOURCES

Sodium and potassium are the two most important alkali metals; they are the sixth and seventh most abundant elements on the planet. Sodium and potassium salts are dissolved in seawater. Sodium makes up more than 1 percent of seawater. Potassium is less common.

TRY THIS

Fizzing rocket

The reactivity of alkali metals can be used to power a homemade rocket. You will need a toilet-paper roll, an empty film canister, a paper plate, some water, and half an indigestion tablet, such as Alkaseltzer.

Tape the toilet-paper roll so it stands upright on the plate. Half fill the canister with water. Put the plate on the ground in an open space outside. Drop the half tablet into the canister and quickly close the lid, making sure it is on tight. Turn the canister upside down and drop it into the toilet-paper roll. Stand back and wait for several seconds. Caution: do not look down the toilet-paper roll.

Soon the canister will launch into the air. The water will spill out into the toilet-paper-roll launcher and plate, so you may need to replace them if you want to repeat the activity several times.

The canister rocket is powered by the reaction between the tablet and the water. The tablet contains sodium bicarbonate, which produces bubbles of carbon dioxide gas when it reacts with water. The gas builds up inside the canister. Eventually the pressure of the gas gets so high that it pushes off the canister's lid so it can escape. As the gas rushes out, it pushes the canister up through the launcher and high into the air.

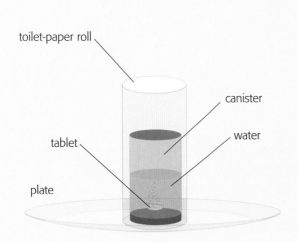

toilet-paper roll

canister

tablet

water

plate

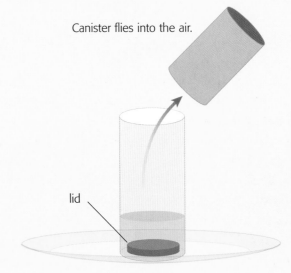

Canister flies into the air.

lid

Compounds of both metals are found in many types of minerals and rocks. The other alkali metals are quite rare. Francium is radioactive so its atoms break apart into other elements. Chemists estimate that there is only 1 ounce (28 g) of francium on Earth at a single point in time.

None of the alkali metals are found as pure elements in nature because they are so reactive. Instead they occur as salts. A salt is a compound formed when an acid reacts with an alkali.

Sodium's most common salt is sodium chloride (table salt). Others include saltpeter (sodium nitrate; $NaNO_3$), which is an ingredient of gunpowder and used to make glass, and borax (sodium borate; $Na_2B_4O_7$), which was once used in soaps.

Potassium chloride (KCl) is that metal's most common salt. Another one is potash (potassium carbonate; K_2CO_3). This is also called salt of tartar. Potash is used to make soft, luxury soaps.

In most cases the alkali metals are purified by electrolysis, a process that breaks salts apart using electricity. The

electrolysis of sodium chloride produces sodium and chlorine atoms. The equation for this process looks like this:

$$2NaCl \rightarrow 2Na + Cl_2$$

USES

The number of industrial uses for the alkali metals is huge. For example, the yellow streetlights you see along major roadways get their color from sodium gas glowing inside. Sodium bicarbonate ($NaHCO_3$), or baking powder, is used to make cakes. The compound reacts with water in the cake mix and releases carbon dioxide gas (CO_2). This gas is trapped as bubbles inside the cake, making it light and spongy.

Alloys of the alkali metals are also very useful. Sodium is used to purify titanium and mercury, while an alloy of sodium and potassium collects the heat produced in nuclear reactors.

▲ *The yellow light of these streetlights is produced by sodium gas. The gas gives out light when an electric current runs through it.*

Key Terms

- **Electron shell:** A layer of electrons that surrounds the nucleus of an atom.
- **Ionic bond:** A bond produced when oppositely charged ions are attracted to each other.
- **Molecule:** Two or more atoms connected together.
- **Salt:** A compound made from positive and negative ions that forms when an alkali reacts with an acid.

See Also ...
Chemical Bonds, Vol. 3: pp. 10–21.

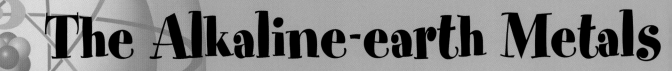

The Alkaline-earth Metals

The alkaline-earth metals are similar to the alkali metals but are harder and less reactive. This group's most familiar member is calcium. Calcium-containing compounds, such as limestone, occur in large amounts in nature.

The elements in the second column of the periodic table, called Group 2, are known as the alkaline-earth metals. These six elements—beryllium (Be), magnesium (Mg), calcium (Ca), strontium (Sr), barium (Ba), and radium (Ra)—were not purified until the 19th century. However, many of their compounds had been known about since much earlier times. For example calcium-containing compounds, such as marble, a type of calcium carbonate ($CaCO_3$), has been used as a building material for thousands or years. As early as the first

Seashells are made of calcium carbonate, a compound that contains an alkaline-earth metal.

Chemistry in Action

Alkaline-earth-metal compounds

Compound	Formula	Common name	Use
Calcium oxide	CaO	Quicklime	Used in building materials
Calcium carbonate	$CaCO_3$	Limestone, calcite	Used in mortar and toothpaste
Calcium sulfate	$CaSO_4$	Gypsum	A fertilizer and fireproofing agent
Magnesium carbonate	$MgCO_3$	Magnesite	Gymnastic chalk
Magnesium hydroxide	$Mg(OH)_2$	Milk of magnesia	Indigestion remedy
Magnesium silicate	$MgSi_4O_{10}$	Soapstone	Talcum powder
Magnesium sulfate	$MgSO_4$	Epsom salts	Laxative

century B.C.E., the Romans were making buildings from concrete that contained quicklime (calcium oxide; CaO).

Alkaline-earth metals are named for these and other compounds. *Earth* is an old name for a naturally occurring compound. Before the study of chemicals became scientific in the 17th century, people thought different earths were elements themselves. They noticed that some of the earths were similar to the alkaline substances such as lye (sodium hydroxide; $NaOH$). They were called alkaline earths. Once it was found that these substances were really compounds containing metals, the metals were named the alkaline-earth metals.

Calcium and magnesium, the two most common alkaline-earth metals were discovered by English chemist Humphry

Davy (1778–1829). He made this discovery in 1807, a year after isolating some of the first alkali metals.

The last member of the group to be discovered was radium, which was isolated by Marie (1867–1934) and Pierre Curie (1859–1906) in 1898. Radium is radioactive so particles break away from its atoms' nuclei. This changes the number of particles in the atom, so

Key Terms

- **Compound:** A substance formed when atoms of two or more different elements bond together.
- **Nucleus:** Central core of an atom.
- **Radioactive:** When an atom has an unstable nucleus that breaks apart.

it becomes an atom of another element. The particles given out by radioactive elements are termed *radiation*.

ATOMIC STRUCTURE

The atoms of alkaline-earth metals have two electrons in their outer shell. These are the valence electrons, which take part in chemical reactions.

To become stable the atoms must give away or share these two electrons. In most cases, the alkaline-earth metals readily give away the two electrons, making them reactive metals.

PROPERTIES

The alkaline-earth metals all have two valence electrons and so have similar properties. Their properties resemble those of the alkali metals, but their behavior is less extreme. Alkaline-earth metals have the following properties:

• **Soft:** They are harder than the alkali metals but still softer and more malleable (flexible) than most other metals.

• **Good conductors:** All of them conduct heat and electricity well.

Chemistry in Action

Hard water

Water that contains the alkaline-earth metals calcium or magnesium is commonly called hard water. The alkaline-earth metals dissolved in hard water react with soap and stop it from forming bubbles.

Hard water comes from deep underground, where it trickles through rocks containing calcium and magnesium compounds.

Removing the metals "softens" the water. Hard water also tastes different from soft water because it contains more minerals.

Hard water produces limescale when it is heated. This chalky substance blocks pipes and coats heating elements in kettles and washing machines. Softening the water removes the scale.

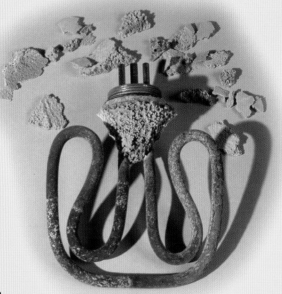

▲ A heating element is coated in limescale from hard water. A layer of limescale stops the element from heating water efficiently.

• **Distinctive colors:** All these metals burn with bright white flames, but when heated they produce light with a certain color. For example, calcium produces dark red flame, strontium a brighter red, and barium produces green flames.

• **Reactive:** Alkaline-earth metals are very reactive but less so that alkali metals. The alkaline-earth metals hold onto their two outer electrons more tightly than the alkali metals hold their one outer electron. The metals become more reactive going down the group.

• **Shiny:** Pure alkaline-earth metals are silver colored and shiny. However, the more reactive members of the group, such as strontium and barium, soon become dull gray. That is because the metals react with oxygen in the air and are covered in a layer of metal oxide.

SOURCES

Calcium and magnesium are the two most common alkaline-earth metals. Calcium makes up about 3 percent of Earth's rocks. It is the third most

▲ The first five alkaline-earth metals, beryllium (1), magnesium (2), calcium (3), strontium (4), and barium (5). Beryllium is the lightest metal in the group and the least reactive. Barium is very dense and the most reactive.

▶ A strip of magnesium burns with a very bright white flame. Magnesium is used in emergency flares because it burns so brightly.

abundant element on the planet. Magnesium makes up about 2 percent of the Earth's rocks and is the eighth most abundant element on the planet. The other alkaline-earth metals are rare. None of the alkaline-earth metals are found as pure elements in nature because they are so reactive.

Calcium occurs mostly in soils as calcium carbonate, an ingredient in limestone. Magnesite, or magnesium carbonate ($MgCO_3$), is one of the most common natural magnesium compounds.

Alkaline-earth metals are purified by electrolysis. This is a process in which a powerful electric current is used to split a compound into its elements (*see* p. 17). Calcium chloride ($CaCl_2$) and magnesium chloride ($MgCl_2$) are used for this process. As well as pure metal, the reaction also produces chlorine gas (Cl_2):

$$CaCl_2 \rightarrow Ca + Cl_2$$

▼ *Cascades of calcium carbonate at Pamukkale in Turkey. These formations are produced by spring water that contains a lot of dissolved calcium minerals.*

BOND FORMATION

Most alkaline-earth metal compounds are ionic. Ionic compounds are formed when one atom loses electrons and another gains them. An alkaline-earth metal atom forms an ion by losing its two outer electrons. This results in an ion with a charge of 2+, which is written as, for example, Ca^{2+}. The lost electrons are picked up by the atoms of another

Key Terms

- **Acid:** A compound that contains large amounts of hydrogen (H^+) ions.
- **Alkali:** A compound that contains large amounts of hydroxide (OH^-) ions.
- **Atom:** The smallest piece of an element that retains the properties of the element.
- **Bond:** An attraction between atoms.
- **Ion:** An atom that has lost or gained one or more electrons.

element. Those atoms become negatively charged ions. Ions with opposite charges are attracted to each other and they bond into a compound.

Pure alkaline-earth metals will react with oxygen (O) in the air to form an ionic compound called an oxide. For example, magnesia (magnesium oxide; MgO) is made up of one magnesium ion (Mg^{2+}) bonded to an oxide ion (O^{2-}). The two electrons given away by the magnesium have been picked up by the oxygen. The equation for this chemical reaction is:

$$2Mg + O_2 \rightarrow 2MgO$$

CHEMICAL REACTIONS

Calcium carbonate ($CaCO_3$) from limestone has many uses. For example, it is used in the production of steel. However, limestone is also turned into a quicklime (CaO) through a simple reaction. When limestone is heated it decomposes into quicklime and carbon dioxide gas (CO_2):

$$CaCO_3 \rightarrow CaO + CO_2$$

Quicklime is a reactive substance. It is an ingredient in plaster, mortar, and cement. When water (H_2O) is added to quicklime, a reaction takes place

TRY THIS

Testing alkalis and acids

Alkaline-earth metals make compounds that are alkaline. You can investigate how they react with an acid using this activity. You will need lemon juice, some milk of magnesia (an indigestion medicine), and indicator paper. Lemon juice is an acid, which contains many hydrogen ions. It turns indicator paper red. Milk of magnesia is magnesium hydroxide, $Mg(OH)_2$, an alkali. It contains many hydroxide ions and turns indicator paper blue.

Begin by testing the juice with a piece of indicator paper. Put the paper on one side to dry so you can compare its color with later tests. Add three tablespoons of milk of magnesia to the juice and stir the mixture. Re-test the liquid with a strip of indicator paper. Compare the color of this strip. It should be less red than the first. This is because the milk of magnesia and some of the acid ions have reacted to produce neutral products.

Keep adding more magnesia and re-testing the mixture. The mixture will gradually lose its acidity and become alkaline. At this point the paper will turn dark green.

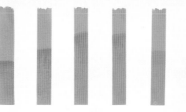

▲ Lemon juice is acidic, but as more and more milk of magnesia is added to the lemon juice, the mixture becomes increasingly alkaline. Testing with indicator paper shows a gradual change from red to dark green.

Chemistry in Action

Body works

Calcium is the most common alkaline-earth metal found in the human body. Two percent of an adult's weight is made up of calcium. Most calcium is in the teeth and bones, in the form of calcium phosphate and calcium carbonate. These compounds make bones and teeth hard.

Water in the human body, such as in the blood and inside cells, contains dissolved calcium ions. The calcium ions are involved in making muscles move and in sending electricity around the brain and along nerves.

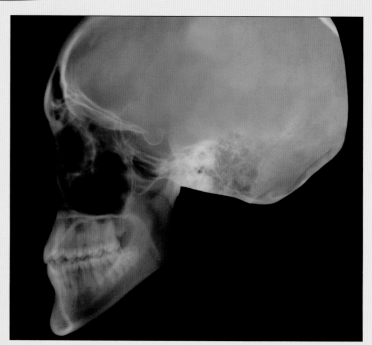

▶ *An X-ray of a person's head shows the hard skull and teeth, which contain calcium compounds.*

▼ *A gymnast swings on a bar. He has a powder on his hands to help him grip. The powder is magnesium carbonate. It is often called "chalk," but it is not the same as the substance used on blackboards.*

that is known as slaking. The reaction produces slaked lime or calcium hydroxide—$Ca(OH)_2$:

$$CaO + H_2O \rightarrow Ca(OH)_2$$

Slaked lime is an alkali—a substance that contains a lot of hydroxide ions (OH^-). Alkalis react with acids, which are compounds that contain a lot of hydrogen ions (H^+).

▶ *Water roars through a dam across the Columbia River in Washington. The dam is made from concrete, a mixture of sand, clay, and calcium compounds, such as quicklime and gypsum. This mixture is a liquid when wet but dries rock hard.*

When quicklime is added to mortar or another building material it is mixed with water. The two compounds react, and the resulting slaked lime then undergoes another reaction. Carbon dioxide in the air dissolves in water inside the mortar to make a carbonic acid (H_2CO_3). This acid reacts with the slaked lime to form calcium carbonate and water. The reaction looks likes this:

$$Ca(OH)_2 + H_2CO_3 \rightarrow CaCO_3 + 2H_2O$$

Calcium carbonate occurs naturally in limestone, and following these reactions the mortar has literally turned to stone.

USES

Alkaline-earth metals have many other uses. Magnesium is alloyed with aluminum to make strong but light objects, such as aircraft. Beryllium is added to copper to make it harder.

Until about 1950 radium was used to make paints that glowed in the dark. The glow came from the radioactive atoms releasing radiation. We now know that radiation of this kind can be harmful to humans. Today radium is only used in safe ways.

Tools and Techniques

Writing on the wall

Teachers use a common calcium compound in the classroom. The chalk used to write on blackboards is a type of limestone, which contains calcium carbonate. Chalk forms from the remains of tiny sea organisms. When they die, their shells, which contain calcium carbonate, build up in piles in shallow waters. Over the years the shells form a thick layer and are squeezed into chalk.

See Also ...
• *What Is Matter?*
  Vol. 1: pp. 4–15.
• *Introducing Elements,*
  Vol. 1: pp. 16–23.

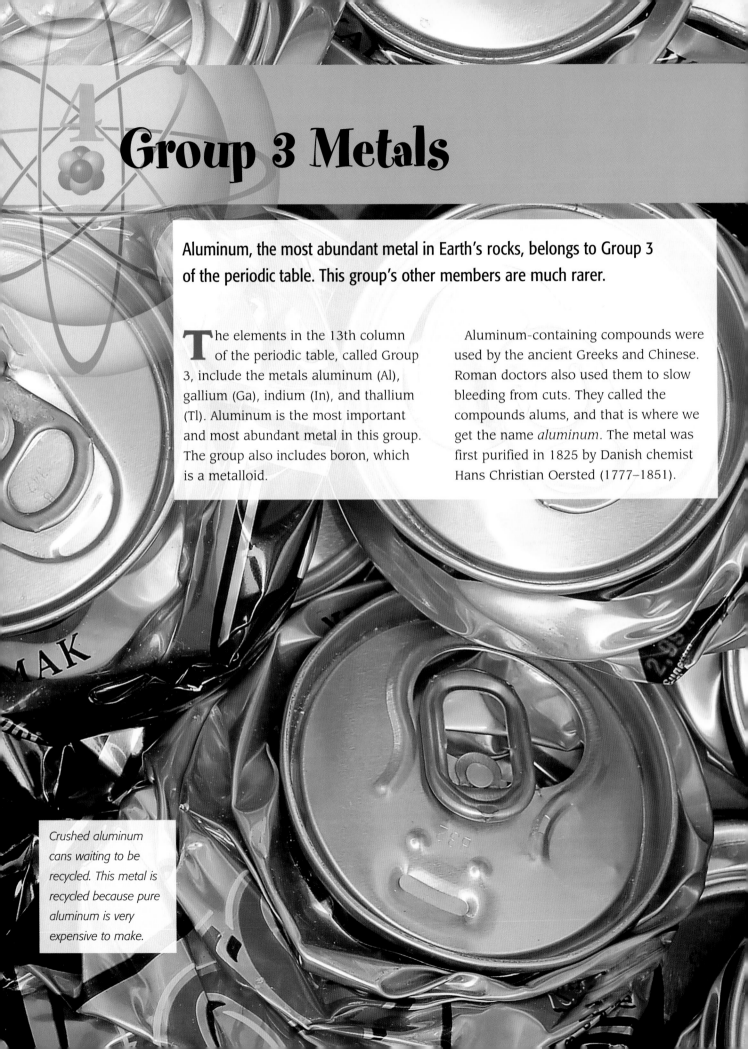

Group 3 Metals

Aluminum, the most abundant metal in Earth's rocks, belongs to Group 3 of the periodic table. This group's other members are much rarer.

The elements in the 13th column of the periodic table, called Group 3, include the metals aluminum (Al), gallium (Ga), indium (In), and thallium (Tl). Aluminum is the most important and most abundant metal in this group. The group also includes boron, which is a metalloid.

Aluminum-containing compounds were used by the ancient Greeks and Chinese. Roman doctors also used them to slow bleeding from cuts. They called the compounds alums, and that is where we get the name *aluminum*. The metal was first purified in 1825 by Danish chemist Hans Christian Oersted (1777–1851).

Crushed aluminum cans waiting to be recycled. This metal is recycled because pure aluminum is very expensive to make.

Chemistry in Action

Group 3 compounds

Compound	Formula	Common name	Use
Aluminum chlorohydrate	$Al_2(OH)_5Cl$	–	Used in deodorants
Aluminum oxide	Al_2O_3	Alumina; corundum	Found in rubies and sapphires
Gallium arsenide	GaAs	–	Produces laser light
Indium phosphide	InP	–	Used in semiconductors
Thallium bromide	TlBr	–	Used in heat detectors
Thallium sulfate	Tl_2SO_4	–	Rat and ant poison

▲ Aluminum foil is as thin as paper so it can be rolled and folded. It is used in cooking, to store food, and as insulation.

Gallium, indium, and thallium were all discovered in the mid-19th century using spectroscopes, instruments that read the unique light pattern produced when materials are heated (see p. 35).

ATOMIC STRUCTURE
All Group 3 metals have three valence electrons in their outer electron shells. To become stable, atoms must give or share these three electrons. Losing three electrons requires a lot more energy than losing one or two. As a result Group 3 metals are only mildly reactive, much less so than alkali metals, for example.

PROPERTIES
Aluminum, gallium, indium, and thallium have many of the classic metal properties. They are all gray or silver in color and shiny. They also conduct heat and electricity very well. However, it is their soft and flexible nature that makes these metals unusual.

Aluminum is the second most malleable (moldable) metal on Earth (second only to gold). Gallium, indium, and thallium are very soft. Each has an unusually low melting point and are nearly liquids in normal conditions.

SOURCES

Aluminum is the most abundant metal in Earth's crust, making up about 7 percent of rocks and minerals. Yet it is one of the most difficult metals on the planet to make in a pure form.

Like most metals, aluminum does not appear in nature as a free element. The main aluminum ore is alumina (aluminum oxide; Al_2O_3). Pure alumina is a colorless and extremely stable compound that takes a lot of energy to split into individual elements. The compound is known also as corundum. It is the main substance in ruby and sapphire gemstones.

Aluminum has only been produced in large amounts for about 100 years. It is purified through a complex process that involves both electrolysis (*see* p. 17) and smelting (*see* p. 53). Today many aluminum objects are made from recycled metal. It takes 20 times less energy to reuse aluminum than it does to purify it.

Gallium, indium, and thallium are rare and found mostly in the ores of other metals, such as copper, zinc, and lead. They are extracted as by-products when these other metals are refined.

▲ *Large passenger aircraft, such as this Boeing 747, are made from aluminum alloys. Aluminum is strong but also very light, making large aircraft light enough to fly.*

BOND FORMATION

The three valence electrons in the outer shells of Group 3 metals are key to how they react with other elements. To become stable, an atom of one of these metals must give away its three electrons to empty its shell.

Most metals bond ionically but the Group 3 elements can also form covalent bonds. An ionic bond is one that forms when ions with opposite charges attract each other. The atoms of Group 3 metals form ions by losing three outer electrons to become, for example, Al^{3+}. These ions are attracted to negatively charged ions, which have gained electrons.

A covalent bond forms when atoms share pairs of electrons instead of giving away or gaining them. By sharing, each atom can fill its outer shell with electrons and become more stable. A few Group 3 compounds, such as aluminum iodide (AlI_3), are covalent. However, most Group 3 metals form ionic compounds.

History

Making pure aluminum

Charles Martin Hall (1863–1914) was a U.S. chemist who invented an inexpensive way of making pure aluminum. Hall made his discovery in 1886 aged just 23. He did his research in a laboratory in his house in Oberlin, Ohio.

The process became known as the Hall-Héroult process because Frenchman Paul Héroult (1863–1914) developed a similar system at the same time. Before the Hall-Héroult process was invented, pure aluminum was as expensive as silver. Although aluminum compounds were common, it was very difficult to refine the metal.

Hall's discovery changed all that and made it possible for aluminum to be used in all kinds of ways. The Hall-Héroult process is still used today. It involves electrolysis, in which an electric current splits alumina (aluminium oxide; Al_2O_3) into pure aluminium and oxygen. This is done at a high temperature so the alumina is melted into a liquid.

▶ *A statue of Charles Martin Hall made from aluminum. The statue belongs to Oberlin College in Ohio, where Hall was a student.*

Key Terms

- **Covalent bond:** A bond in which atoms share electrons.
- **Ionic bond:** A bond produced when oppositely charged ions are attracted to each other.
- **Malleable:** Describes a material that can be bent easily or pounded into a flat sheet.
- **Molecule:** Two or more atoms connected together.
- **Metalloid:** A substance with the properties of both a metal and a nonmetal.
- **Ore:** A mineral that contains valuable amounts of a metal.
- **Refine:** To purify a metal by removing unwanted elements.

Alumina (Al_2O_3) is a typical example of an ionic compound. It forms when aluminum comes in contact with the oxygen (O_2) in the air. The equation for the chemical reaction is:

$$4Al + 3O_2 \rightarrow 2Al_2O_3$$

In each molecule of alumina, two Al^{3+} ions are bonded to three O^{2-} ions.

Alumina forms as a thin layer on the surface of the metal. That stops oxygen from getting to the pure metal underneath so the reaction cannot continue.

Gallium, indium, and thallium are all more reactive than aluminum. As the metal with the largest atoms, thallium is the most reactive (*see* p. 18). It must be stored underwater to prevent it from reacting with oxygen in the air.

CHEMICAL REACTIONS

Aluminum is often used as a reducing agent. A reducing agent is a compound that gives away electrons during a chemical reaction. Aluminum is the reducing agent for an important reaction called the thermite process.

This reaction is used to make pure iron from iron oxide (Fe_2O_3). The aluminum atoms give electrons to the iron ions (Fe^{3+}) during the reaction. As a result the aluminum atoms become ions (Al^{3+}) and bond to the oxide ion (O^{2-}) to form alumina. The Fe^{3+} ions become atoms of pure iron. The reaction looks like this:

$$Fe_2O_3 + 2Al \rightarrow Al_2O_3 + 2Fe$$

Common chemical reactions of gallium, indium, and thallium are harder to describe, partly because they are rare. Gallium can corrode other metals—a chemical reaction in which one metal oxidizes another.

USES

Aluminum is one of the most useful metals on Earth. Not since iron replaced bronze as the most useful metal at the dawn of the Iron Age has a metal been

▼ *Gallium's melting point is 86°F (30°C). The heat from a hand is enough to turn gallium into a liquid.*

Tools and Techniques

Studying light

Many rare metal elements were discovered using a tool called a spectroscope. Spectroscopes use a triangular lens called a prism to split light into different colors. When it is heated or burned, each element produces light containing a unique set of colors. When light from a flame is split into colors by a spectroscope, chemists can see what elements are involved in the reaction. Some of the Group 3 metals produce interesting colors. For example, indium is named for the bright indigo color seen in the light it emits.

▶ *White light contains all the colors of the rainbow. A prism separates these colors.*

Chemistry in Action

Poison plan

A 1967 report shows that the U.S. Central Intelligence Agency (CIA) discussed poisoning the Cuban dictator Fidel Castro (1926–) with thallium compounds. The plan was to put powder in Castro's shoes when they were being polished. There would be just enough poison to make Castro ill and for his hair and beard to fall out. The CIA hoped this would make him look bad in public. Though the plan was never used, thallium sulfate is used as a poison for rats and other pests.

more important. Although iron is still the most-used metal, aluminum's properties make it useful in different ways. For example, it is light and so is used to make aircraft and electricity cables that are hung from pylons. It is also malleable and can be molded into many shapes. Perhaps the most common shape is that of an aluminum can.

Most aluminum products are alloys (mixtures of metals). Small amounts of copper, zinc, magnesium, and silicon are added to it to make it harder.

Alumina is used to protect steel (an iron alloy) from rusting. A thin layer of the compound is coated on the steel. The coating stops oxygen and moisture from getting to the iron underneath.

See Also ...
● *Metals and Metallurgy, Vol. 10: pp. 22–37.*

Tin and Lead

Tin and lead are familiar metals because they have been used by people for many thousands of years. Both are easy to purify and are unreactive and so are often used to protect other metals from damage.

Model soldiers made of an alloy of tin and lead. The alloy is easy to melt and pour into molds.

The metals tin (Sn) and lead (Pb) appear in the 14th column of the periodic table, which is known as Group 4. Tin and lead are the only metals in this group. The other Group 4 elements are germanium and silicon, which are classed as metalloids, and carbon, which is a nonmetal.

People have used tin and lead for 7,000 years. Tin was added to copper to make the alloy bronze. Lead was bent into tubes and other useful shapes.

No one knows who first discovered and named these metals. Their chemical symbols come from their Latin names—*stannum* for tin, and *plumbum* for lead.

It is easy to make pure tin and lead. Rocks sometimes contain pure lead. However neither of the metals is very common in nature.

ATOMIC STRUCTURE

The atoms of tin and lead each have four valence electrons in their outer shell. To become stable, these atoms need eight or no electrons in their outer shells. That can be achieved by losing four electrons or gaining four. Both options require a lot of energy. As a result tin and lead are not very reactive elements, and they are not involved in many chemical reactions with other elements.

While the four valence electrons make tin and lead fairly unreactive, they also enable the atoms to form very stable bonds. A stable bond is one that is not easily broken. Once a tin or lead atom bonds with another element, that bond is very hard to break.

Tin and lead are described as "poor metals" because they do not react in the same way as other metals. The only metals that are less reactive than tin and lead are the so-called precious metals, such as gold and platinum.

PROPERTIES

The atomic structure of tin and lead helps create an important characteristic of both elements—the ability to resist corrosion. Corrosion is a chemical reaction between a metal and its environment, usually the oxygen and water in the air, which weakens the metal. Rusting is a type of corrosion.

▲ *Small rings of molded tin. When it is cold, tin is easy to bend but becomes more likely to break when it is heated. Most metals are easier to bend when warm.*

Key Terms

- **Alloy:** A metallic substance that contains two or more metallic elements.
- **Electron shell:** A layer of electrons that surrounds the nucleus of an atom.
- **Valence electrons:** The outermost electrons of an atom, which are involved in chemical reactions.

Chemistry in Action

Compounds and alloys of tin and lead

Compound/Alloy	Formula	Common name	Use
Lead acetate	$Pb(C_2H_3O_2)_2$	Sugar of lead	A poisonous, sugarlike substance used in dyes and varnish
Lead carbonate	$2PbCO_3$	White lead	A white pigment (coloring)
Lead oxide	PbO	Litharge	Once used to make yellow paint and glass
Lead tetraoxide	Pb_3O_4	Red lead	A red pigment
Niobium-tin	Nb_3Sn	–	A superconductor that conducts electricity very well
Bronze	60% Cu, 40% Sn	–	An alloy containing tin (Sn) and copper (Cu)
Pewter	85% Sn, 15% Pb	–	A substitute for silver once used to make shiny objects
Solder	60% Sn, 40% Pb	–	An alloy used to fuse metals
Tin tetrachloride	$SnCl_4$	Stannic chloride	Used to toughen glass

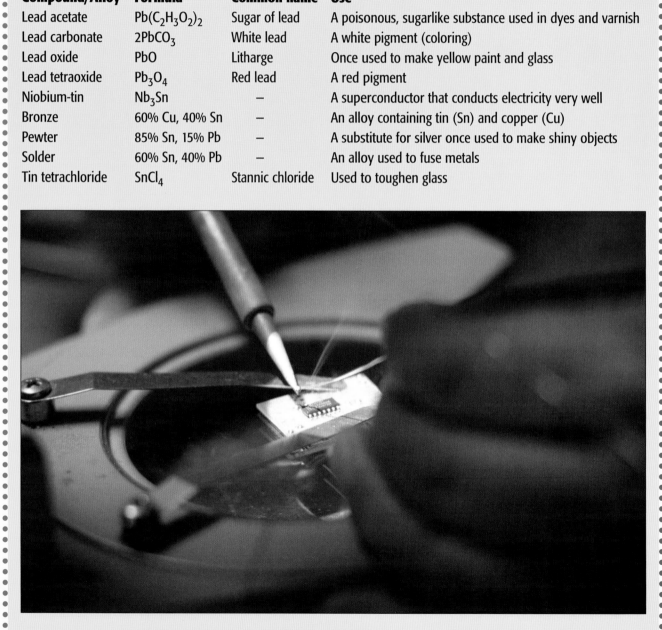

▲ A microchip is soldered into place. The solder (right) is an alloy of tin and lead. It is melted by a hot soldering iron (left). The melted alloy flows around the chip. The solder cools and becomes solid again, holding the chip in place.

Tin and lead do not rust because they react only slowly with oxygen to form oxides. Like other lead and tin compounds, the oxides are very stable. They form a thin layer on the surface of the metals. This layer acts as a barrier between the air and the metal, which prevents any more reactions from taking place.

Tin and lead also share other properties. Both are soft metals that can be bent or molded easily. They have low melting and boiling points compared to other metals. Both are also poor conductors of electricity and heat compared to other metals.

SOURCES

Both tin and lead occur only in very small quantities in Earth's crust. If you took a random scoop of one million pieces, or parts, of the Earth's crust, only two parts would be tin and twelve parts would be lead. Scientists call this way of measuring parts per million, or ppm. In this case, the Earth's crust is 2 ppm tin and 12 ppm lead.

Tin occurs as ores—minerals that contain a useful amount of the metal. Much of the world's tin is contained in the mineral cassiterite, which is mainly tin oxide (SnO_2). Cassiterite tends to be located in soft ground close to the surface. As a result it is mined using the open-pit method. Some mines have tunnels leading down to the ore. However, an open-pit mine is just a huge hole dug into the ground. The largest tin mines are in Malaysia.

Lead is sometimes found as a pure metal, especially near volcanoes where the heat causes minerals to react. Most lead is found in the form of the mineral

A Closer LOOK

Lead poisoning

People have used lead for many thousands of years, but only recently did we learn that lead can damage the human nervous system and cause blood and brain disorders.

Today, lead has been removed from paints, gasoline, and ceramics to protect people from its harmful effects. However, lead was a common cause of illness in the past. For example, lead is thought to have made many Romans insane. They used lead water pipes and even added lead to their food as a sweetener.

German composer Ludwig van Beethoven (1770–1827) may have also been poisoned by lead. Lead could could have gotten into his body through eating fish and drinking wines sweetened with lead, and using pewter dishes. Beethoven was also often ill with stomach problems. When he died doctors found that his organs were damaged in a way that might have been caused by lead.

▲ Caligula (12–41 C.E.) was an insane Roman emperor. He made his horse the leader of his government. The emperor's mental illness may have been a result of lead poisoning.

galena (lead sulfide; PbS). Galena and other lead ores are generally located deep underground in hard rocks. The metal is also found in the ores of other metals, such as silver and copper.

CHEMICAL REACTIONS

Having four valence electrons makes tin and lead unreactive metals. To form a bond with another atom, the tin or lead atom must give away its four outer electrons and become an ion. An ion is an atom that has lost or gained electrons and has become charged as a result. Tin and lead atoms form ions with a charge of 4+. Losing four electrons requires a lot of energy, which is why tin and lead do not react easily.

Ions are attracted to other ions with an opposite charge. This attraction forms bonds between the ions and creates an ionic compound. For example, tin ions (Sn^{4+}) bond to two oxide ions (O^{2-}) to form casserite (SnO_2). Galena (PbS) is one lead ion (Pb^{4+}) bonded to one sulfide ion (S^{4-}).

Pure tin and lead are removed from their compounds by reacting them with carbon (C). This is a displacement reaction in which the carbon takes the place of

Can man

▲ Tin cans from 1899 that still contain food.

French inventor Nicolas François Appert (1750–1841) invented a way of keeping food fresh by storing it in airtight containers. He invented this process in 1809 for the French emperor Napoleon Bonaparte. Napoleon wanted a way for his army to carry food without it going bad. Appert put raw food in glass jars sealed with corks. He then boiled the jars until the food inside was cooked. This process killed all the bacteria that could rot the food. In 1811 a British company started to use metal cans instead of jars. The cans did not break as easily. The metal used was iron coated in a layer of tin to stop it from rusting—the tin can was born.

◀ Galena is the most common lead-containing compound in nature.

the metal in the compound. The reaction requires heat, which is supplied by burning the carbon. (Coal is a fuel made of mainly carbon.) For example, tin is extracted from cassiterite, in a chemical reaction that looks like this:

$$SnO_2 + 2C \rightarrow 2CO + Sn$$

▶ *Gasoline used to have lead compounds in it to help it burn evenly. However, the lead came out in the exhaust fumes and damaged people's health. Today most gasoline is unleaded.*

USES

Tin and lead have many uses. Tin is used to protect other metals from rusting. Food cans are coated with a layer of tin for this reason. They are still referred to as tin cans in some parts of the world, although most of the metal in them is steel (a strong alloy of iron containing carbon and other elements).

Tin is also a common ingredient in alloys. Bronze, pewter, and solder all contain large proportions of tin. Pewter and solder also contain lead.

Lead is used a lot less than tin because it is poisonous. However, it is used to make ammunition, glass, ceramics, brass, and cable covers. As a very heavy metal, lead is used in weights. More than half of the lead used today comes from recycled products.

Key Terms

- **Compound:** A substance formed when atoms of two or more different elements bond together.
- **Conductor:** A substance that carries electricity and heat well.
- **Ion:** An atom that has lost or gained an electron or electrons.
- **Mineral:** A naturally occurring compound, such as those that make up rocks and soil.
- **Ore:** A mineral that contains valuable amounts of a metal.

BS 7070 Pre

See ALSO ...
● *Chemistry and the Environment, Vol. 10: pp. 38–51.*

Transition Metals

Nearly half of all metals are transition elements. These metals form a block across the center of the periodic table. Many of the most common and familiar metals, such as copper, iron, and gold, are transition metals.

The elements between the third and twelfth columns of the periodic table are called the transition series. This block contains about 30 elements, all of which are metals.

The transition metals include some metals that have been known about for thousands of years, such as iron (Fe), silver (Ag), and copper (Cu). The other metals in the series have been discovered over the past 300 years. Transition metals with lower atomic numbers (*see* vol 1: pp. 24–35), and therefore with smaller and lighter atoms, were generally discovered before the elements with larger, heavy atoms. Heavy metals tend to be more reactive than lighter ones, thus are more difficult to isolate from compounds.

Many gemstones are colored by transition metals. Chromium makes emeralds green and rubies red, while titanium makes sapphires blue.

Widely used transition metals include manganese (Mn), chromium (Cr), cobalt (Co), nickel (Ni), tungsten (W), and titanium (Ti). The rarer transition metals include molybdenum (Mo), palladium (Pd), rhodium (Rh), and zirconium (Zr).

ATOMIC STRUCTURE

The transition metals form a series rather than a group. That is because they all share an unusual atomic structure that separates them from all other metals. However, they also have a varying number of outer electrons, so they cannot be formed into a group in the same way as other metals. Nevertheless, like most of the other groups of metals, transition metals have just one or two electrons in their outermost electron shells. These electrons are valence electrons and so are involved in chemical reactions with other elements.

With one or two outer electrons, transition elements react in the same way as alkali metals (*see* p. 14) and alkaline-earth metals (*see* p. 22). The

▲ *Some of the largest human-made objects in the world, such as this tanker, are made from steel—an alloy containing mainly iron.*

Chemistry in Action

▲ Many sun-protection creams contain zinc oxide, a white substance that blocks ultraviolet light. Ultraviolet (UV) light is invisible radiation that is produced by the Sun. UV radiation can damage the skin causing sunburn and tanning. Zinc oxide is used to make space suits UV-proof. It is also used to make white paints and inks.

Transition-metal compounds

Compound	Formula	Common name	Use
Brass	67% Cu, 33% Zn	–	Alloy used to make ornaments and musical instruments
Cobalt oxide	CoO	Cobalt blue	A deep blue compound used to color glass and china
Copper sulfate	$CuSO_4$	–	Used as a pesticide
Hematite	Fe_2O_3	Black diamond	The main iron ore
Lead chromate	$PbCrO_4$	Chrome yellow	A bright yellow pigment
Manganese dioxide	MnO_2	Pyrolusite	Used in batteries
Stainless steel	90% Fe, 10% Cr	–	Used to make shiny objects that do not rust
Vanadium pentoxide	V_2O_5	–	A catalyst used to produce sulfuric acid

Alkali metals

H

Li Be — Alkaline-earth metals

Na Mg — Transition metals

Nonmetals He

B C N O F Ne

Al Si P S Cl Ar

K Ca Sc Ti V Cr Mn Fe Co Ni Cu Zn Ga Ge As Se Br Kr

Rb Sr Y Zr Nb Mo Tc Ru Rh Pd Ag Cd In Sn Sb Te I Xe

Cs Ba La Hf Ta W Re Os Ir Pt Au Hg Ti Pb Bi Po At Rn

Fr Ra Ac

Rare-earth metals

Ce Pr Nd Pm Sm Eu Gd Tb Dy Ho Er Tm Yb Lu

Th Pa U Np Pu Am Cm Bk Cf Es Fm Md No Lr

▲ *The transition metals form the middle block of the periodic table. The term* transition, *which means "to change from one thing to another," is used because the block connects the two sides of the table.*

transition metals are generally less reactive than these other groups. We find the reason for this by looking more closely at the elements' atomic structures. As well as in the outer electron shell, transition elements also have valence electrons in the next shell in toward the nucleus.

LAYERS OF ELECTRON

An atom's electrons are arranged in shells that fit inside one another (*see* p. 8). The smallest and innermost shell contains just two electrons. The second shell is larger and can hold up to eight

(*see* p. 8)

Key Terms

- **Alloy:** A metallic substance that contains two or more metallic elements.
- **Electron shell:** A layer of electrons that surrounds the nucleus of an atom.
- **Metal:** A substance that is solid, shiny, moldable, and that can carry electricity.
- **Ore:** A naturally occurring substance that contains valuable amounts of a metal.
- **Valence electron:** One of the outer electrons in an atom that is involved in chemical reactions.

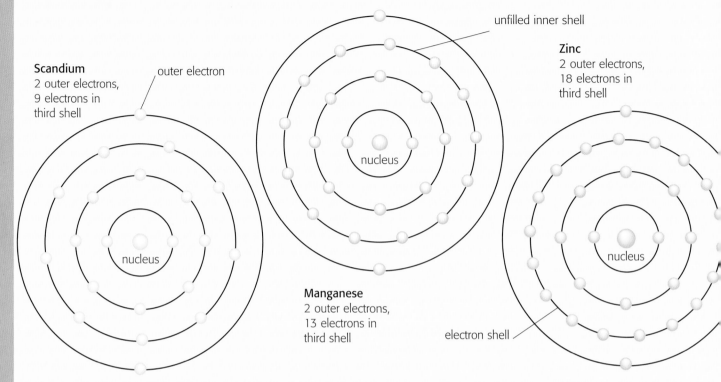

Scandium
2 outer electrons,
9 electrons in
third shell

outer electron

unfilled inner shell

nucleus

Zinc
2 outer electrons,
18 electrons in
third shell

nucleus

Manganese
2 outer electrons,
13 electrons in
third shell

electron shell

nucleus

electrons. The third shell is larger still and has room for up to 18 electrons. However, instead of filling up with this number of electrons, once the third shell has eight electrons, it stops accepting any more. The fourth shell then begins to fill up. The story does not end there. Once the fourth shell has two electrons, the third shell begins to accept electrons again.

ADDING ELECTRONS

To illustrate this, let us compare the atomic structures of calcium and scandium. Calcium is the last element in the periodic table before the transition series begins. Scandium is the first member of the series. Calcium

▶ *A piece of zinc. Zinc is one of the most reactive of the transition metals.*

▲ *Like most metals, the transition metals have one or two outer electrons. However, the next shell in can have anything from 8 to 18 electrons. These inner electrons also take part in reactions.*

atoms have four shells. The third shell has eight electrons, and the fourth has two. Scandium atoms also have four shells. As in calcium, the fourth shell has two electrons, but the third shell has nine.

The third shell continues to fill up producing a series of metal atoms with four electron shells. Most of these atoms have two outer electrons, although a few such as chromium and copper have one.

The third shell is finally full in the atoms of zinc, where it contains 18 electrons. At this point the fourth and outer shell begins to fill up again.

Following zinc, atoms of the metal gallium form. Gallium is not a transition metal. Its atoms have a third shell with 18 electrons, and a fourth shell with three electrons.

The fourth shell continues to gain electrons until it holds eight in the atoms of the gas krypton. As happened with the third shell, the fourth shell now stops accepting any more electrons. A fifth electron shell begins to form. Once this shell holds two electrons, the fourth shell beneath it then continues to fill. Another series of metal atoms with five shells and one or two outer electrons is formed. The same process also occurs in atoms with six shells. The transition series ends with mercury (Hg).

PROPERTIES

Transition metals tend to be good conductors and they are the toughest metals, with much higher melting points than the metals in other groups. However,

▷ *Mercury is the only metal that is liquid in normal conditions. Its chemical symbol is Hg. That comes from the the Latin word* hydrargyrum, *which means "water silver."*

▽ *A bridge made of steel, an alloy of iron and carbon with other metals mixed in. Steel is extremely strong but can also be molded and bent.*

Copper sulfate

Cobalt chloride

Chromium chloride

Nickel nitrate

Iron chloride

there are some notable exceptions. For example, mercury is liquid at room temperature, and gold is very malleable.

Many of the elements' properties are the result of how their atoms bond together. In most cases, the transition metals have a lot of valence electrons. As well as being involved in reactions, these also help form metallic bonds (*see* p. 10). The more electrons metal atoms use to form these bonds, the stronger they will be. Having strong bonds between its atoms makes a metal very hard. The strong bonds hold each

▲ *Transition-metal compounds are often brightly colored. Chromium produces especially colorful compounds. The name* chromium *comes from* chroma, *the Greek word for "color."*

Key Terms

- **Conductor:** A substance that carries electricity and heat well.
- **Compound:** Atoms of different elements bonded together.
- **Density:** A measure of how tightly atoms are packed into a solid.
- **Malleable:** When a material can be bent easily or pounded into a flat sheet.
- **Metallic bond:** A bond between a group of metal atoms that are sharing a pool of electrons.

atom in a fixed position, and it takes a large force to break them apart or push them into a different shape. However, many hard transition metals, such as iron and chromium, are also brittle. That is, when they do break they shatter into pieces. These metals are made less brittle by being alloyed with other substances.

The strong bonds also make the metal atoms pack tightly together, and as a result some transition metals are very dense. Measuring a substance's density is a way of comparing how big it is (volume) with how heavy it is (weight). A handful of a dense substance weighs more than the same volume of a less

▼ *An assortment of batteries. Batteries contain transition metals such as nickel, cadmium, and manganese. They are involved in reactions that produce electric currents (see vol. 3: p. 50).*

Tools and Techniques

Measuring temperature

We take advantage of mercury being a liquid at everyday temperatures in a tool used to measure temperature: the thermometer. This instrument was invented in 1592. It is a hollow glass tube marked with the temperature and filled with mercury. As it gets warm, the mercury expands and moves up the glass tube, indicating a change in temperature. Today, mercury thermometers are only used under controlled conditions because the metal is extremely poisonous.

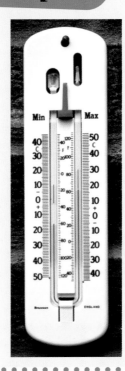

▶ *A mercury thermometer designed to measure a day's maximum (right) and minimum (left) temperatures.*

dense substance. The densest element of all is the transition metal osmium (Os). A cube of this metal with sides measuring 1 inch weighs a surprising 13 ounces (22.5 g/cm^3). That is 22.5 times heavier than the same volume of water.

The strong bonds also result in high melting and boiling points because it takes a lot of energy to break the bonds. Most transition metals melt at temperatures above 1,832°F (1,000°C). Tungsten has the highest melting point of any metal: 6,192°F (3,422°C).

SOURCES

A few transition metals, such as mercury, gold, and platinum, are found pure in nature. Others occur in minerals combined with other elements. Useful

metals, such as iron and copper, are extracted from such minerals, which are called ores. Ores are minerals that contain large amounts of a valuable metal. Other transition metals are rare and are not refined from their own ores. Instead they are produced as by-products when more common metals are being produced.

Key Terms

- **By-product:** A substance that is produced when another material is made.
- **Earth's crust:** The layer of solid rock that covers the surface of Earth.
- **Melting point:** The temperature at which a solid substance melts into a liquid.
- **Mineral:** A natural compound, such as those that make up rocks and soil.

▼ A vast pit created by digging copper ore from the ground.

◄ *A crystal of hematite. This mineral is a compound containing iron and oxygen. Hematite is the main ore of iron.*

The other transition metals that are mined for their ores are nickel, zinc, and titanium. Of these transition metals, titanium is the ninth most abundant and zinc is the 23rd most abundant element in Earth's crust. Nickel and copper are not far behind.

The ores are generally found near the surface, so they are dug up directly from the surface, creating huge holes or pits in the process.

The ores of iron and other transition metals are refined to make pure metals using a process called smelting (*see* box, p. 53). In this process metal oxides are reacted with carbon (C). During the reaction the carbon takes oxygen out of the ore, leaving pure metal behind.

Iron is the planet's most common element. Scientists think that Earth's core is a huge ball of hot iron and nickel (another transition metal). However, only about 5 percent of the Earth's crust is iron, making it the fourth most abundant element in rocks. Most iron occurs bonded to oxygen to make compounds called iron oxides.

▶ *Transition metals with atomic numbers 104 to 112 are artificial elements made in laboratories. They are made by chemists fusing smaller atoms. These metals are named for famous scientists. Rutherfordium, for example, is named for Ernest Rutherford, the New Zealand chemist who discovered the atomic nucleus. Rutherford is seen here on the left photographed in 1908.*

Rarer transition metals are purified in the same way, generally as by-products. For example, rhodium is a by-product of nickel production, and cadmium is a by-product of zinc refining.

VALENCE ELECTRONS

The atomic structure of transition metals has a great effect on how these elements form bonds with other elements. Atoms bond to each other by giving, taking, or sharing their valence electrons. The atoms do this to fill or empty their outer electron shells.

The transition metals have valence electrons in two electron shells rather than just the outer one like most other elements. So the way their atoms use these electrons to form bonds with other atoms is far more complicated.

Most of the nontransition elements must lose, gain, or share a fixed number of electrons in order to become stable and form a bond. However, transition metals can form compounds by using a varying number of their valence electrons. That makes the chemical behavior of

▲ *These test tubes contain solutions of four different copper compounds. Each solution has a different color because copper has bonded in a different way.*

transition metals so complex. In many cases, an atom of a transition metal can form three or four different compounds with atoms of another element.

OXIDATION STATES

Chemists figure out how a transition element forms its bonds by calculating something called the oxidation state.

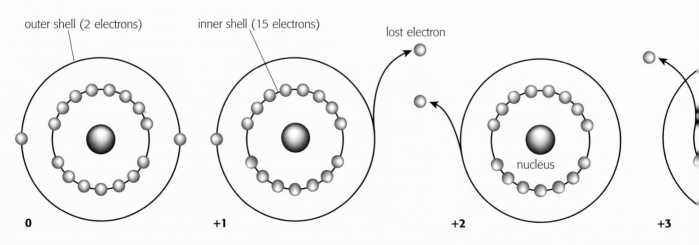

outer shell (2 electrons)   inner shell (15 electrons)   lost electron   nucleus

0   +1   +2   +3

Increase in oxidation number

Despite its name, the oxidation state is just a number that tells chemists how many electrons an atom has lost or gained as it formed a compound with other elements. For example, when the nontransition metal magnesium (Mg) reacts with the nonmetal oxygen (O_2), it loses its two valence electrons. As a result it forms an ion with a charge of 2+ (Mg^{2+}). An ion is an atom that has lost or gained an electron and so has become charged. The oxygen gains two electrons to fill its outer shell and forms the negatively charge ion O^{2-}. In this example the magnesium has an oxidation state of +2, while the oxygen has a state of −2.

Most transition metals can have more than one oxidation state. For example, those of manganese are +7, +4, +3, and +2. In other words, manganese atoms can lose up to seven electrons

There are four types of cobalt ions, each one with a certain oxidation state. The oxidation number goes up each time the cobalt loses an electron.

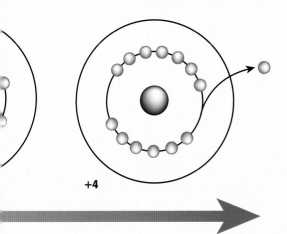

+4

Tools and Techniques

▲ *Molten (liquid) iron is poured from a giant ladle into molds.*

Purifying metals

Many metals are purified from their ores by a process called smelting. Iron is the main metal to be smelted, but manganese, cobalt, and nickel are also purified in this way.

Smelting is a series of chemical reactions in which the ore reacts with carbon (C) and then carbon monoxide (CO). The products of the reactions are pure metal, carbon dioxide (CO_2), and waste, known as slag. The reaction's chemical equation looks like this:

$$2Fe_2O_3 + 3C \rightarrow 4Fe + 3CO_2$$

Evidence of iron smelting dates back thousands of years but no one knows who discovered the technique. Today, iron smelting takes place in a chimney-shaped blast furnace. Iron ore is heated with coke, a type of coal that is almost pure carbon. The ore melts and reacts with the carbon to produce carbon monoxide. This gas also reacts and removes the last of the oxygen from the ore to produce pure molten (melted) iron and carbon dioxide. Oxygen is also blasted through the mixture to burn away impurities.

during a reaction. That is more than any other metal. Iron has the oxidation states of +3 and +2, while copper's are +2 and +1.

A few transition metals have just one oxidation state. For example, scandium's is +3, and zinc only forms ions with a oxidation state of +2.

FORMING BONDS

The oxidation state of a transition metal tells chemists how many ions are needed to make a compound. Like most other metals, transition metals make ionic compounds. These are produced when ions bond together. Ions are attracted to other ions with an opposite charge. This attraction is what creates a bond between the two ions.

While the ions that make up a compound are charged, the compound itself is neutral—it does not have a charge. That is because the opposite charges of the ions balance each other. So the oxidation state, or charge, of a transition-metal ion determines how many ions it bonds with.

▼ A man holds a gauze made from wires of the transition metals rhodium and platinum. The gauze is used as a catalyst during the production of nitric acid. A catalyst triggers or speeds up a reaction without itself being changed.

Chemistry in *Action*

Metals in the blood

Iron is vital in blood because it bonds with oxygen. The iron is part of a large molecule called hemoglobin. This molecule makes our blood red. Hemoglobin picks up oxygen molecules that are breathed into the lungs and then carries them throughout the body. However, not all animals use iron for this purpose. The king crab, which is an ocean-living relative of scorpions and spiders, uses copper compounds instead of iron ones to transport oxygen around in its body. The crab's blood is blue owing to the copper.

▶ *A magnified image of blood cells traveling through a blood vessel. The cells are red because they contain a lot of hemoglobin.*

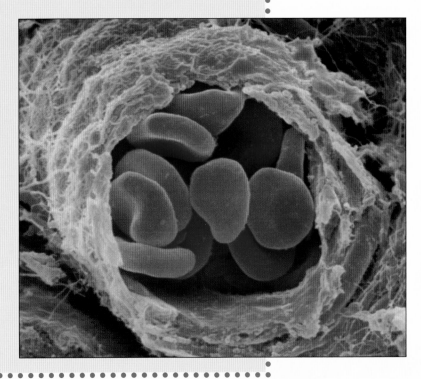

For example, when copper has an oxidation state of +1 (Cu^+) it takes two ions to form a compound with an oxygen ion (O^{2-}). The compound has the formula Cu_2O. Chemists call this compound cuprous oxide, or copper (I) oxide—the "I" is "one" in Roman numbers. When copper has an oxidation state of +2 (Cu^{2+}) it forms cupric oxide—copper (II) oxide (CuO).

HELPING REACTIONS

The transition metals are often good catalysts. A catalyst is something that makes a chemical reaction go faster. One example, known as the Haber process, uses iron (Fe) to make ammonia (NH_3).

The chemical reaction looks like this:

$$N_2 + 3H_2 \xrightarrow{Fe} 2NH_3$$

Putting its symbol above the arrow shows that the iron is the catalyst and not a reactant or product. The iron plays a part in the reaction but is not used up by it. In this example, the iron catalyst gives and takes electrons (changing its oxidation state), so the nitrogen (N) and hydrogen (H) atoms have more chances to bond with each other.

Another reason transition metals are good catalysts is because other substances can stick to their surfaces. While the substances are stuck, atoms can rearrange to form new chemical substances. One chemical reaction that uses a transition-metal catalyst in this way converts small organic (carbon-based) chain molecules into larger ones. For example, ethane (C_2H_4) reacts with hydrogen (H_2) to become propane (C_3H_6) when heated in the presence of a nickel catalyst.

A metal catalyst that works in this way adsorbs the other atoms. Notice that this word does not have the same meaning as *absorb*. When something is absorbed it becomes mixed into another substance. When it is *adsorbed,* a substance clings to the surface of another, but remains separate.

DIFFERENT USES

Transition metals are the metals used in industry to make everything from rust-proof roofs to earrings. However, many

of the metals are also important for the chemical reactions that take place inside living bodies. Without tiny amounts of several transition metals in their bodies, people would become ill.

As we have seen, an iron compound is used in our blood to transport oxygen. It also makes blood red. Human bodies use other transition metals in similar ways. Several are ingredients of vitamins. Cobalt, for example, is a vital part of vitamin B12, which occurs naturally in meat, eggs, and dairy products. The body also needs minute amounts of chromium, manganese, copper, zinc, and several other transition elements to stay healthy. However, if people eat large amounts of these metals they will become ill.

▲ *These rings are made from platinum. Platinum is a precious metal, along with gold and silver. These transition metals do not react very easily, so they do not rust or tarnish quickly and stay shiny and clean for long periods. They are described as precious because they are rare metals and therefore expensive.*

Key Terms

- **Catalyst:** An element or compound that helps a chemical reaction occur more quickly but that is not altered by the reaction.
- **Ion:** An atom that has lost or gained one or more electrons.
- **Ionic bond:** A bond produced between oppositely charged ions.
- **Oxidation state:** A number used to describe how many electrons an atom has lost or gained.

▶ *A close-up of a crystal of vitamin B12. This compound contains cobalt. B12 is also called cobalamin and is essential for good health. People who do not have enough vitamin B12 have problems with their blood.*

▼ *A shiny taillight on a car from the 1950s. This metal fitting is made from chrome, which is steel coated in a layer of chromium. The chromium protects the steel from rusting, keeping the metal shiny and reflective.*

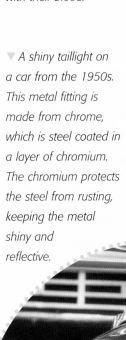

TRY THIS

Iron in food

Many foods have iron added to them to make them healthful. You can extract the iron from breakfast cereal. You will need some cereal flakes, a Ziploc bag, a cup of water, plastic food wrap, a paper towel, and a small magnet taped to a wooden stick. Seal some flakes in the bag and crush them into a fine powder. Pour the powder into a bowl and mix it with the water. Stir the mixture of cereal for 10 minutes with the magnet covered in plastic food wrap. Wipe the food wrap with a paper towel. You should see tiny specks of black powder on the towel–the iron in your cereal. Repeat with other cereals and compare the amount of iron you find.

Key Terms

- **Magnet:** A piece of iron, nickel, or cobalt that produces a magnetic force.
- **Molecule:** Two or more connected atoms.
- **Organic:** Describing a compound that is made of carbon and hydrogen.
- **Vitamin:** A substance that is essential for good health.

In industry, iron is the most important of all metals. It is easy to find and inexpensive to refine. About 95 percent of all the pure metal produced each year is iron. In its pure form, iron is very brittle and not very useful. However when it is alloyed with a small amount of carbon it becomes a flexible and strong alloy called steel.

Many of the other transition metals are rarely used in their pure form. Instead they are mixed with iron to make steels

▲ A five-cent coin, or nickel, is made from an alloy of nickel and copper. The coin was introduced in 1866 as an alternative to coins made of silver.

with different properties. For example, chromium is added to make stainless steel, which does not rust. Steel containing molybdenum is very hard. Steel with a coating of zinc is called galvanized steel. This alloy is also rust-proof and is often used outdoors.

Transition metals that are used on their own include gold, silver, and titanium, which is both stronger and lighter than steel. Copper is a good conductor and is used to make electric wires. Zinc, cadmium, and nickel are used in batteries.

MAGNETISM

Three transition metals—iron, cobalt, and nickel—can be made into magnets. A magnet is an object that has two poles, known as north and south. When two magnets come together, the like poles repel each other, while opposite poles attract. The magnetic force that does this is produced by the electrons spinning inside the atoms of these three metals. No other elements, metal or nonmetal, can be used to make magnets.

An electromagnet picks up scrap iron at a junkyard. Electromagnets are magnets that can be turned on and off. They only work when an electric current runs through them.

See Also ...
- *The Metals, Vol. 5: pp. 34–43.*
- *Metals and Metallurgy, Vol. 10: pp. 22–37.*

Metalloids

The metalloids are the most unusual of all elements. They have properties of both metals and nonmetals. Many metalloids are semiconductors, which are substances used in electronics, such as computers and cell phones.

The metalloids, also known as the semimetals, are elements that have both metal and nonmetal properties. These six elements—boron (B), silicon (Si), germanium (Ge), arsenic (As), antimony (Sb), and tellurium (Te)—form a jagged diagonal line separating the metals from the nonmetals on the periodic table. Polonium (Po), a radioactive element, is also sometimes considered a metalloid.

Arsenic and antimony have been used for thousands of years. Arsenic was commonly used as a poison and to make glass. Ancient Egyptians used poisonous antimony compounds in eye makeup. The other metalloids were discovered from the late 18th through the 19th century.

The metalloids blend metallic and nonmetallic properties. Some are hard and slightly shiny; others are crumbly

A circuit board with microchips and other electronics that contain metalloids, such as silicon and arsenic.

powders. A few conduct electric currents while others block them. In addition, unlike metals, metalloids are brittle and shatter easily.

ATOMIC STRUCTURE

The metalloids belong to several groups in the periodic table—from column 13 to column 16. As a result metalloids have a variety of atomic structures.

Boron has three electrons in its outermost shell; silicon and germanium have four outer electrons; arsenic and antimony have five outer electrons;

▶ *The purity of a sample of gallium arsenide is tested before it is used to make a superconductor, which conducts electricity very efficiently.*

Metalloid compounds

Compound	Formula	Common name	Use
Antimony trioxide	Sb_2O_3	–	A fireproofing agent
Silicon dioxide	SiO_2	Silica or sand	Used to make glass and concrete
Sodium borate	$Na_2B_4O_7$	Borax	A component of soaps, cleaners, and bleach
Sodium silicate	Na_4SiO_5	Silica gel	A drying agent
Gallium arsenide	GaAs	–	Used in solar cells and lasers
Germanium tetrahydride	GeH_4	Germane	Used to make semiconductors
Cadmium zinc telluride	CdZnTe	–	An alloy used in radiation detectors and to make holograms
Lead arsenate	$PbHAsO_4$	–	An insecticide

Key Terms

- **Metal:** A hard but flexible element. Metals are good conductors. Their atoms have only a few outer electrons.
- **Metalloid:** An element that has both metallic and nonmetallic properties.
- **Nonmetal:** An element that is not a metal or metalloid. Nonmetals are poor conductors. Their atoms tend to have several outer electrons.

tellurium and polonium have six valence electrons. These different atomic structures influence the properties of the metalloids considerably.

▲ *Pure arsenic takes two forms. This powder is yellow arsenic, which looks like a nonmetal. Gray arsenic is shiny and looks more like a metal.*

PROPERTIES

As a result of their varying atomic structures, there are no properties shared by all metalloids. Instead some metalloids are more metallic than others,

while some are more nonmetallic. For example, pure germanium and polonium look more like metals than other metalloids, while boron and arsenic are more nonmetallic. Most metalloids exist in two forms when pure—one metallic, the other nonmetallic.

SOURCES

Silicon is perhaps the most important metalloid. It is the second most abundant element in Earth's crust. (Oxygen is the most common element.) Silicon makes up more than a quarter of Earth's rocks and minerals.

Silicon is never found uncombined in nature. Its most common compound is with oxygen—silicon dioxide (SiO_2). This substance is commonly called silica and it is perhaps most familiar as the tiny crystals that make up sand. Silica also occurs in other forms, which go by other names. Quartz is a form of silica that is found in many rocks, such as granite. Flint is another form of the compound found in rocks. Many precious stones are colored forms of silica, including jasper, opal, agate, and onyx.

Metalloid	Appearance	Conductivity
Boron	Metallic and nonmetallic forms	Insulator
Silicon	Metallic and nonmetallic forms	Semiconductor
Germanium	Metallic	Semiconductor
Arsenic	Metallic and nonmetallic forms	Semiconductor
Antimony	Metallic	Semiconductor
Tellurium	Nonmetallic	Insulator
Polonium	Metallic	Insulator

Boron has two main sources, the minerals borax and kernite. Both are forms of sodium borate ($Na_2B_4O_7$). The largest deposits of these minerals are underneath Boron, California, a town named for the metalloid.

Minerals containing the other metalloids do not exist in large amounts. Antimony occurs as a sulfide mineral called stibnite (SbS_3). However, stibnite is rarely used to refine pure antimony. Antimony is made mainly as a by-product of silver and lead production. Tellurium is a common impurity in gold, lead, and copper. Germanium is also a by-product

Although silicon compounds are very easy to find, the other metalloids are not. They almost always occur bound to other elements. In many cases, the metalloids are produced as by-products when refining other metals.

Arsenic commonly occurs as arsenopyrite (FeAsS), a compound of iron (Fe), arsenic (As), and sulfur (S). Because arsenic is poisonous and has few uses, it is not usually extracted from this ore. Instead, arsenic is a by-product in the treatment of other metals.

▲ A woman who has been poisoned by arsenic in her well water. The arsenic has covered her hands with green blisters.

▶ A crystal of quartz, which is a natural form of silica. Quartz is one of the most common minerals in rocks. Sand is made up of tiny grains of quartz.

Key Terms

- **Conductor:** A substance that carries electricity and heat well.
- **Electricity:** A stream of charged particles moving through a substance.
- **Insulator:** A substance that does not carry an electric current or heat.

of refining these metals and also zinc. Radioactive polonium is produced when radium breaks down (decays; *see* p. 23). Polonium itself decays into lead.

BOND FORMATION

All the metalloids except boron have four or more valence electrons in their outermost shell. Because they need eight electrons to become stable, the metalloids most often get the extra outer electrons to fill their shells by sharing them with other atoms. This sharing forms covalent bonds.

Silica (SiO_2), the most common metalloid-containing compound, is held together by covalent bonds. The reaction that produces silica looks like this:

$$Si + O_2 \rightarrow SiO_2$$

▷ *A piece of gallium arsenide, a compound of the metal gallium and arsenic. This material is used to make very fast-working microchips. Microchips are made in clean, dust-free conditions, so this person is wearing a suit and mask so he does not add impurities.*

Chemistry in Action

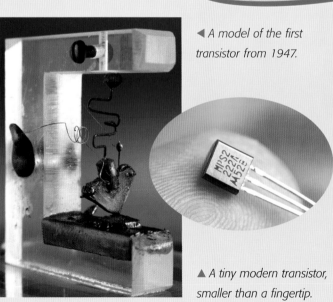

◀ *A model of the first transistor from 1947.*

▲ *A tiny modern transistor, smaller than a fingertip.*

Electronics center

Silicon Valley is an area of northern California. Many of the world's microchips are made there. The area is so called because silicon is the most common material used in microchips. Silicon and some other metalloids are semiconductors. They conduct electricity only in certain conditions. This property makes them very useful for making electronic devices, such as transistors and diodes, which are used in computers and other machines. Transistors are switches that direct current around a circuit. Diodes are devices that allow current to travel in just one direction. Microchips contain tiny transistors, diodes, and other electronics.

However, the way atoms bond to form silica is more complicated than this equation shows. An oxygen atom has to share two electrons with other atoms to become stable. A silicon atom has four electrons to share. In silica each oxygen atom gets its two electrons from two silicon atoms and is bonded to both of them. Although its formula is SiO_2, each silicon atom is bonded to four oxygens. Silica's bonds connect all the atoms in a vast network, or lattice. That makes it a very hard and stable compound.

USES

The most important use of metalloids is in semiconductors. Silicon and germanium are the main semiconducting metalloids. Other metalloids, such as arsenic, are added to semiconductors in tiny amounts to adjust their properties. This process is called doping.

Semiconductors are substances that conduct electricity in the presence of energy such as heat, light, or electrical energy. For example, thermistors are semiconductors influenced by heat. They are used in thermometers and thermostats. Light-sensitive semiconductors are used in solar cells, which generate electricity from sunlight, and photoreceptors, which detect light. Digital cameras take pictures by recording the image formed on photoreceptors behind the lens.

Computers and similar machines are controlled by semiconductors that are influenced by electric currents. These devices act as switches and mechanisms that work together in large numbers to carry out complex tasks (*see* box, p. 64).

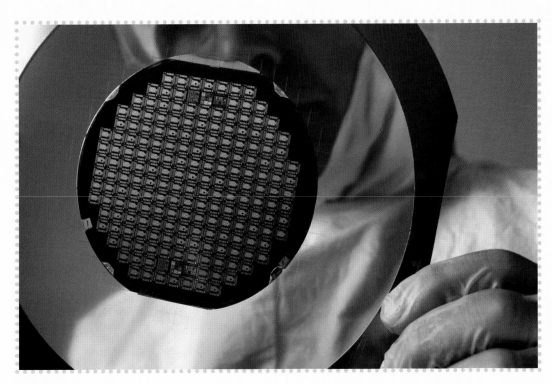

◄ *A thin wafer of silicon with electronic components etched on its surface. The wafer will be cut up into chips.*

See Also ...

• *Chemical Bonds, Vol. 3: pp. 10–21.*
• *The Metalloids, Vol. 5: pp. 56–61.*

More Information

BOOKS

Atkins, P. W. *The Periodic Kingdom: A Journey into the Land of Chemical Elements.* New York, NY: Basic Books, 1997.

Bendick, J., and Wiker, B. *The Mystery of the Periodic Table (Living History Library).* Bathgate, ND: Bethlehem Books, 2003.

Berg, J., Stryer, L., and Tymoczko, J. *Biochemistry.* New York, NY: W. H. Freeman, 2002.

Brown, T., Burdge, J., Bursten, B., and LeMay, E. *Chemistry: The Central Science.* 10th ed. Englewood Cliffs, NJ: Prentice Hall, 2005.

Cobb, C., and Fetterolf, M. L. *The Joy of Chemistry: The Amazing Science of Familiar Things.* Amherst, NY: Prometheus Books, 2005.

Cox, M., and Nelson, D. *Lehninger's Principles of Biochemistry.* 4th ed. New York, NY: W. H. Freeman, 2004.

Davis, M. *Modern Chemistry.* New York, NY: Henry Holt, 2000.

Herr, N., and Cunningham, J. *Hands-on Chemistry Activities with Real Life Applications.* Hoboken, NJ: Jossey-Bass, 2002.

Houck, Clifford C., and Post, Richard. *Chemistry: Concepts and Problems.* Hoboken, NJ: Wiley, 1996.

Karukstis, K. K., and Van Hecke, G. R. *Chemistry Connections: The Chemical Basis of Everyday Phenomena.* Burlington, MA: Academic Press, 2003.

LeMay, E. *Chemistry: Connections to Our Changing World.* New York, NY: Prentice Hall (Pearson Education), 2000.

Oxlade, C. *Elements and Compounds.* Chicago, IL: Heinemann, 2002.

Poynter, M. *Marie Curie: Discoverer of Radium* **(Great Minds of Science)**. Berkeley Heights, NJ: Enslow Publishers, 2007.

Saunders, N. *Fluorine and the Halogens.* Chicago, IL: Heinemann Library, 2005.

Shevick, E., and Wheeler, R. *Great Scientists in Action: Early Life, Discoveries, and Experiments.* Carthage, IL: Teaching and Learning Company, 2004.

Stwertka, A. *A Guide to the Elements.* New York, NY: Oxford University Press, 2002.

Tiner, J. H. *Exploring the World of Chemistry: From Ancient Metals to High-Speed Computers.* Green Forest, AZ: Master Books, 2000.

Trombley, L., and Williams, F. *Mastering the Periodic Table: 50 Activities on the Elements.* Portland, ME: Walch, 2002.

Walker, P., and Wood, E. *Crime Scene Investigations: Real-life Science Labs for Grades 6–12.* Hoboken, NJ: Jossey-Bass, 2002.

Wertheim, J. *Illustrated Dictionary of Chemistry* (Usborne Illustrated Dictionaries). Tulsa, OK: Usborne Publishing, 2000.

Wilbraham, A., et al. *Chemistry.* New York, NY: Prentice Hall (Pearson Education), 2000.

Woodford, C., and Clowes, M. *Routes of Science: Atoms and Molecules.* San Diego, CA: Blackbirch Press, 2004.

WEB SITES

The Art and Science of Bubbles
www.sdahq.org/sdakids/bubbles
*Information and activities
about bubbles.*

Chemical Achievers
www.chemheritage.org/classroom/
chemach/index.html
*Biographical details about leading
chemists and their discoveries.*

The Chemistry of Batteries
www.science.uwaterloo.ca/~cchieh/
cact/c123/battery.html
Explanation of how batteries work.

The Chemistry of Chilli Peppers
www.chemsoc.org/exemplarchem/
entries/mbellringer
*Fun site giving information on the
chemistry of chilli peppers.*

The Chemistry of Fireworks
library.thinkquest.org/15384/
chem/chem.htm
*Information on the chemical
reactions that occur when
a firework explodes.*

The Chemistry of Water
www.biology.arizona.edu/
biochemistry/tutorials/chemistry/
page3.html
*Chemistry of water and other
aspects of biochemistry.*

Chemistry: The Periodic Table Online
www.webelements.com
Detailed information about elements.

Chemistry Tutor
library.thinkquest.org/2923
*A series of Web pages that help
with chemistry assignments.*

Chem4Kids
www.chem4Kids.com
*Includes sections on matter, atoms,
elements, and biochemistry.*

Chemtutor Elements
www.chemtutor.com/elem.htm
*Information on a selection of
the elements.*

Eric Weisstein's World of Chemistry
scienceworld.wolfram.com/
chemistry
*Chemistry information divided into
eight broad topics, from chemical
reactions to quantum chemistry.*

General Chemistry Help
chemed.chem.purdue.edu/genchem
*General information on chemistry
plus movie clips of key concepts.*

Molecular Models
chemlabs.uoregon.edu/
GeneralResources/models/
models.html
*A site that explains the use
of molecular models.*

New Scientist
www.newscientist.com/home.ns
*Online science magazine providing
general news on scientific
developments.*

Periodic Tables
www.chemistrycoach.com/periodic_
tables.htm#Periodic%20Tables
*A list of links to sites that have
information on the periodic table.*

The Physical Properties of Minerals
mineral.galleries.com/minerals/
physical.htm
Methods for identifying minerals.

**Understanding Our Planet Through
Chemistry**
minerals.cr.usgs.gov/gips/
aii-home.htm
*Site that shows how chemists
and geologists use analytical
chemistry to study Earth.*

Scientific American
www.sciam.com
*Latest news on developments
in science and technology.*

Snowflakes and Snow Crystals
www.its.caltech.edu/~atomic/
snowcrystals
*A guide to snowflakes, snow
crystals, and other ice
phenomena.*

Virtual Laboratory: Ideal Gas Laws
zebu.uoregon.edu/nsf/piston.html
*University of Oregon site showing
simulation of ideal gas laws.*

What Is Salt?
www.saltinstitute.org/15.html
Information on common salt.

Periodic Table

The periodic table organizes all the chemical elements into a simple chart according to the physical and chemical properties of their atoms. The elements are arranged by atomic number from 1 to 116. The atomic number is based on the number of protons in the nucleus of the atom. The atomic mass is the combined mass of protons and neutrons in the nucleus. Each element has a chemical symbol that is an abbreviation of its name. In some cases, such as potassium,

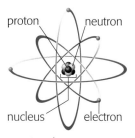

proton   neutron

nucleus   electron

Atomic structure

33	Atomic (proton) number
As	Chemical symbol
Arsenic	Element name
75	Atomic mass

☐ HYDROGEN
▨ ALKALI METALS
▨ ALKALINE-EARTH METALS
☐ METALS
▨ LANTHANIDES

Transition metals

	Group 1	**Group 2**	**Group 3**	**Group 4**	**Group 5**	**Group 6**	**Group 7**	**Group 8**	**Group 9**
Period 1	1 **H** Hydrogen 1								
Period 2	3 **Li** Lithium 7	4 **Be** Beryllium 9							
Period 3	11 **Na** Sodium 23	12 **Mg** Magnesium 24							
Period 4	19 **K** Potassium 39	20 **Ca** Calcium 40	21 **Sc** Scandium 45	22 **Ti** Titanium 48	23 **V** Vanadium 51	24 **Cr** Chromium 52	25 **Mn** Manganese 55	26 **Fe** Iron 56	27 **Co** Cobalt 59
Period 5	37 **Rb** Rubidium 85	38 **Sr** Strontium 88	39 **Y** Yttrium 89	40 **Zr** Zirconium 91	41 **Nb** Niobium 93	42 **Mo** Molybdenum 96	43 **Tc** Technetium (98)	44 **Ru** Ruthenium 101	45 **Rh** Rhodium 103
Period 6	55 **Cs** Cesium 133	56 **Ba** Barium 137	Lanthanides	72 **Hf** Hafnium 179	73 **Ta** Tantalum 181	74 **W** Tungsten 184	75 **Re** Rhenium 186	76 **Os** Osmium 190	77 **Ir** Iridium 192
Period 7	87 **Fr** Francium 223	88 **Ra** Radium 226	Actinides	104 **Rf** Rutherfordium (263)	105 **Db** Dubnium (268)	106 **Sg** Seaborgium (266)	107 **Bh** Bohrium (272)	108 **Hs** Hassium (277)	109 **Mt** Meitnerium (276)

rare-earth elements

Lanthanides

Actinides

57 **La** Lanthanum 39	58 **Ce** Cerium 140	59 **Pr** Praseodymium 141	60 **Nd** Neodymium 144	61 **Pm** Promethium (145)
89 **Ac** Actinium 227	90 **Th** Thorium 232	91 **Pa** Protactinium 231	92 **U** Uranium 238	93 **Np** Neptunium (237)

the symbol is an abbreviation of its Latin name ("K" stands for *kalium*). The name by which the element is commonly known is given in full underneath the symbol. The last item in the element box is the atomic mass. This is the average mass of an atom of the element.

Scientists have arranged the elements into vertical columns called groups and horizontal rows called periods. Elements in any one group all have the same number of electrons in their outer shell and have similar chemical properties. Periods represent the increasing number of electrons it takes to fill the inner and outer shells and become stable. When all the spaces have been filled (Group 18 atoms have all their shells filled) the next period begins. Further explanation of the periodic table is given in Volume 5.

ACTINIDES

NOBLE GASES

NONMETALS

METALLOIDS

Group 18

Group 13	Group 14	Group 15	Group 16	Group 17	Group 18
					2 **He** Helium 4
5 **B** Boron 11	6 **C** Carbon 12	7 **N** Nitrogen 14	8 **O** Oxygen 16	9 **F** Fluorine 19	10 **Ne** Neon 20
13 **Al** Aluminum 27	14 **Si** Silicon 28	15 **P** Phosphorus 31	16 **S** Sulfur 32	17 **Cl** Chlorine 35	18 **Ar** Argon 40

Group 10 | Group 11 | Group 12 | | | | | |
---|---|---|---|---|---|---|---|---
28 **Ni** Nickel 59 | 29 **Cu** Copper 64 | 30 **Zn** Zinc 65 | 31 **Ga** Gallium 70 | 32 **Ge** Germanium 73 | 33 **As** Arsenic 75 | 34 **Se** Selenium 79 | 35 **Br** Bromine 80 | 36 **Kr** Krypton 84
46 **Pd** Palladium 106 | 47 **Ag** Silver 108 | 48 **Cd** Cadmium 112 | 49 **In** Indium 115 | 50 **Sn** Tin 119 | 51 **Sb** Antimony 122 | 52 **Te** Tellurium 128 | 53 **I** Iodine 127 | 54 **Xe** Xenon 131
78 **Pt** Platinum 195 | 79 **Au** Gold 197 | 80 **Hg** Mercury 201 | 81 **Tl** Thallium 204 | 82 **Pb** Lead 207 | 83 **Bi** Bismuth 209 | 84 **Po** Polonium (209) | 85 **At** Astatine (210) | 84 **Rn** Radon (222)
110 **Ds** Darmstadtium (281) | 111 **Rg** Roentgenium (280) | 112 **Uub** Ununbium (285) | 113 **Uut** Ununtrium (284) | 114 **Uuq** Ununquadium (289) | 115 **Uup** Ununpentium (288) | 116 **Uuh** Ununhexium (292) | |

artificial elements

62 **Sm** Samarium 150	63 **Eu** Europium 152	64 **Gd** Gadolinium 157	65 **Tb** Terbium 159	66 **Dy** Dysprosium 163	67 **Ho** Holmium 165	68 **Er** Erbium 167	69 **Tm** Thulium 169	70 **Yb** Ytterbium 173	71 **Lu** Lutetium 175
94 **Pu** Plutonium (244)	95 **Am** Americium (243)	96 **Cm** Curium (247)	97 **Bk** Berkelium (247)	98 **Cf** Californium (251)	99 **Es** Einsteinium (252)	100 **Fm** Fermium (257)	101 **Md** Mendelevium (258)	102 **No** Nobelium (259)	103 **Lr** Lawrencium (260)

Glossary

acid Substance that dissolves in water to form hydrogen ions (H^+). Acids are neutralized by alkalis and have a pH below 7.

alkali Substance that dissolves in water to form hydroxide ions (OH^-). Alkalis have a pH greater than 7 and will react with acids to form salts.

alkali metals Those metals that form Group 1 of the periodic table.

alkaline-earth metals Those metals that form Group 2 of the periodic table.

allotrope A different form of an element in which the atoms are arranged in a different structure.

alloy A metallic substance that contains two or more metals. An alloy may also be made of a metal and a small amount of a nonmetal. Steel, for example, is an alloy of iron and carbon.

alumina Aluminum oxide, Al_2O_3. The most common aluminum ore.

amalgams Alloys that contain mercury.

anion Negatively charged ion.

atom The smallest independent building block of matter. All substances are made of atoms.

atomic mass The number of protons and neutrons in an atom's nucleus.

atomic number The number of protons in a nucleus.

base Any substance that produces hydroxide ions, OH^-, is a base. All alkalis are bases.

boiling point The temperature at which a liquid turns into a gas.

bond A chemical connection between atoms.

brass An alloy of copper and zinc.

bronze Alloy made of copper and tin.

by-product A substance that is produced when another material is made.

catalyst A substance that speeds up a chemical reaction but is left unchanged at the end of the reaction.

cation A positively charged ion.

chemical equation Symbols and numbers that show how reactants change into products during a chemical reaction.

chemical formula The letters and numbers that represent a chemical compound, such as "H_2O" for water.

chemical reaction A process in which atoms of different elements join or break apart to form new substances.

chemical symbol The letters that represent a chemical, such as "Cl" for chlorine or "Na" for sodium.

combination reaction A reaction in which two or more reactants combine to form one product.

combustion The reaction that causes burning. Combustion is generally a reaction with oxygen in the air.

compound Substance made from more than one element and which has undergone a chemical reaction.

compress To reduce in size or volume by squeezing or exerting pressure.

conductor A substance that carries electricity and heat.

corrosion The slow wearing away of metals or solids by chemical attack.

covalent bond Bond in which atoms share one or more electrons.

crystal A solid made of regular repeating patterns of atoms.

crystal lattice The regular repeated structure found in crystalline solids.

density The mass of substance in a unit of volume.

deposit A mineral vein or ore inside another rock.

displacement reaction A reaction that occurs when a more reactive atom replaces a less reactive atom in a compound.

dissolve To form a solution.

doping Process by which the properties of semiconductors are adjusted by adding tiny amounts of metalloids.

ductile Describes materials that can be stretched into a thin wire. Many metals are ductile.

elastic Describes a substance that returns to its original shape after being stretched.

electricity A stream of electrons or other charged particles moving through a substance.

electrolysis A method of separating elements in ionic compounds by dissolving the compound in an appropriate solvent and passing an electric current through the solution.

electrolyte Liquid containing ions that carries a current between electrodes.

electron A tiny negatively charged particle that moves around the nucleus of an atom.

electronegativity The power of an atom to attract an electron. Nonmetals, which have only a few spaces in their outer shell, are the most electronegative. Metals, which have several empty spaces in their outer shell, are the least electronegative elements. These metals tend to lose electrons in chemical reactions. Metals of this type are termed electropositive.

element A material that cannot be broken up into simpler ingredients. Elements contain only one type of atom.

energy level The electron shells of an atom each represent a different energy level. Those closest to the nucleus have the lowest energy.

galena Lead sulfide (PbS). Most common mineral containing lead.

geologist Scientist who studies rocks and minerals.

group A column of related elements in the periodic table.

Hall-Héroult process Process for producing large quantities of aluminum.

hematite A compound of iron and oxygen. Hematite is the most common iron ore.

hydrogen bond A weak dipole attraction that always involves a hydrogen atom.

insulator A substance that does not transfer an electric current or heat.

intermolecular bonds The bonds that hold molecules together. These bonds are weaker than those between atoms in a molecule.

intramolecular bond Strong bond between atoms in a molecule.

ion An atom that has lost or gained one or more electrons.

ionic bond Bond in which one atom gives one or more electrons to another atom.

ionic compound Compound made of ionized atoms.

ionization The formation of ions by adding or removing electrons from atoms.

isotope Atoms of a given element must have the same number of protons but can have different numbers of neutrons. These different versions of the same element are called isotopes.

liquid Substance in which particles are loosely bonded and are able to move freely around each other.

lubricant A substance that helps surfaces slide past each other.

magnet A piece of iron, nickel, or cobalt that produces a magnetic force.

malleable Describes a material that can be hammered into different shapes without breaking. Metals are malleable.

melting point The temperature at which a solid changes into a liquid. When a liquid changes into a solid, this same temperature is called the freezing point.

metal An element that is solid, shiny, malleable, ductile, and conductive.

metallic bond Bond in which outer electrons are free to move in the spaces between the atoms.

metalloid Elements that have properties of both metals and nonmetals.

metallurgy The science and technology of metals and their alloys, including methods of extraction and use.

microprocessor A tiny silicon chip that contains all the electronic circuits used to run a computer.

mineral A naturally occurring compound, such as those that make up rocks and soil.

mole The amount of any substance that contains the same number of atoms as in 12 grams of carbon-12 atoms. This number is 6.022 x 10^{23}.

molecule Two or more bonded atoms that form a substance with specific properties.

neutron One of the particles that make up the nucleus of an atom. Neutrons do not have any electric charge.

nucleus The central part of an atom. The nucleus contains protons and neutrons. The exception is hydrogen, which contains only one proton.

ore A mineral that contains valuable amounts of materials such as copper, sulfur, or tin.

oxide Compound that includes oxygen.

oxidation state A number used to describe how many electrons an atom has lost or gained.

periodic table A table of elements arranged by increasing atomic number (proton number).

phase change A change from one state to another.

potash Potassium carbonate (K_2CO_3). Contains potassium, carbon, and oxygen.

pressure The force produced by pressing on something.

proton A positively charged particle found in an atom's nucleus.

quartz A crystalline form of silica, silicon dioxide (SiO_2).

reactivity The tendency of an element to react chemically with other elements.

reducing agent A compound that gives away electrons during a chemical reaction.

refine To purify a metal by getting rid of other unwanted elements.

relative atomic mass A measure of the mass of an atom compared with the mass of another atom. The values used are the same as those for atomic mass.

rare-earth metals Metals that form two rows of elements— the actinides and the lanthanides—below the main body of the periodic table.

relative molecular mass The sum of all the atomic masses of the atoms in a molecule.

salt A compound made from positive and negative ions that forms when an alkali reacts with an acid.

semiconductor A substance that conducts heat and electricity but only in certain circumstances.

shell The orbit of an electron. Each shell can contain a specific number of electrons and no more.

smelting Method for purifying metals from their ores.

solid State of matter in which particles are held in a rigid arrangement.

specific heat capacity The amount of heat required to change the termperature of a specified amount of a substance by 1°C (1.8°F).

standard conditions Normal room temperature and pressure.

state The form that matter takes—either a solid, a liquid, or a gas.

steel An alloy of iron and carbon.

subatomic particles Particles that are smaller than an atom.

temperature A measure of how fast molecules are moving.

transition metals Those metals that make up groups 3 through 12 of the periodic table.

valence A measure of the number of bonds an atom can form with other atoms.

valence electrons The electrons in the outer shell of an atom.

voltage The force that pushes electrons through an electric circuit.

Index

Numbers in **bold** type refer to volume numbers.